teach yourself®

knitting
sally walton

For over 60 years, more than
50 million people have learnt over
750 subjects the **teach yourself**
way, with impressive results.

be where you want to be
with **teach yourself**

For UK order enquiries: please contact Bookpoint Ltd, 130 Milton Park, Abingdon, Oxon, OX14 4SB. Telephone: +44 (0) 1235 827720. Fax: +44 (0) 1235 400454. Lines are open 09.00–17.00, Monday to Saturday, with a 24-hour message answering service. Details about our titles and how to order are available at www.teachyourself.co.uk

For USA order enquiries: please contact McGraw-Hill Customer Services, PO Box 545, Blacklick, OH 43004-0545, USA. Telephone: 1-800-722-4726. Fax: 1-614-755-5645.

For Canada order enquiries: please contact McGraw-Hill Ryerson Ltd, 300 Water St, Whitby, Ontario, L1N 9B6, Canada. Telephone: 905 430 5000. Fax: 905 430 5020.

Long renowned as the authoritative source for self-guided learning – with more than 50 million copies sold worldwide – the **teach yourself** series includes over 500 titles in the fields of languages, crafts, hobbies, business, computing and education.

British Library Cataloguing in Publication Data: a catalogue record for this title is available from the British Library.

Library of Congress Catalog Card Number: on file.

First published in UK 2006 by Hodder Education, 338 Euston Road, London, NW1 3BH.

First published in US 2006 by The McGraw-Hill Companies, Inc.

This edition published 2006.

The **teach yourself** name is a registered trade mark of Hodder Headline.

The publisher has used its best endeavours to ensure that the URLs for external websites referred to in this book are correct and active at the time of going to press. However, the publisher and the author have no responsibility for the websites and can make no guarantee that a site will remain live or that the content will remain relevant, decent or appropriate.

Typeset by Pantek Arts Ltd, Maidstone, Kent.
Printed in Dubai for Hodder Education, a division of Hodder Headline, 338 Euston Road, London, NW1 3BH, by Cox and Wyman Ltd, Reading, Berkshire.

Impression number   10 9 8 7 6 5 4 3 2 1

Year   2010 2009 2008 2007 2006

contents

acknowledgements

A very big thank you to the knitters who helped me with this book: Jane Scruton, Tisha Dunn, Jilly Sillem, Lois Waldron and Debra Cocks.

Thanks also to the good people at Rowan Yarns, Sirdar and Twilleys of Stamford for supplying yarns and equipment for the photographs.

And thanks to Michelle Garrett for her beautiful photographs and to her assistant, Lisa, for her technical wizardry.

Gratitude to my family for putting up with my continuing obsession with knitting.

01 introduction

In this chapter you will learn:

- about the history of knitting
- how to use this book
- about types of knitting equipment
- about different materials.

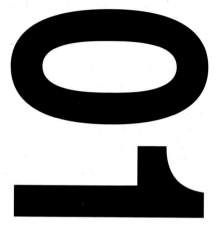

introduction

History of knitting

Amazing but true – there was life on earth before knitting! It is impossible to tell who had the idea first but we can assume that it was nomadic tribes who herded animals and spun yarn from their fleeces. Everyday knitted garments would have been worn until they fell apart, so all ancient fragments that remain are those of fine ceremonial relics and we can only guess the real history of domestic knitting.

There is evidence to suggest that knitting originated in Arab countries as knitted items have been found in Egyptian burial chambers. In fact, the discovery of an unusual sock divided at the big toe seems to prove that Englishmen were not the first to wear socks with sandals! Peruvians were spinning llama and alpaca knitting wool and dying it brilliant colours long before Europeans arrived to 'civilize' the South American continent. Some of the earliest knitting of all was a type of fringing made for the edges of woven cloth in pre-Columbian Peru. The Nazca tribes who lived there thousands of years ago developed a pattern style that involved many bright colour changes to depict human and animal forms.

A knitting Madonna is featured in a 15th-century Italian painting, which suggests that knitting was a familiar Renaissance pastime, and knitting guilds were set up during the Middle Ages in England to produce and trade in high-quality knitted garments. These guilds were made up of groups of highly skilled male knitters and the only women ever allowed to join were the widows of members who had died.

The invention of the knitting frame, and, later, a machine capable of producing hundreds of pairs of identically perfect stockings, signalled the decline of hand knitting, although it remained popular in isolated communities.

Women knitted in a different style, using a knitting sheath or stick at the waist to hold one of the needles rigidly next to the body. A decorative carved sheath was a favourite courtship present given by a young man to his sweetheart. Knitting patterns were not written down but taught and handed down from mother to daughter, often as closely guarded family secrets. When fishermen sailed to other ports, patterns were exchanged or surreptitiously copied by local knitters. It has been only relatively recently that the value of these folk arts and crafts has been appreciated by a wider audience than the communities who traditionally practised them. Folklore tells of each fishing port having its own pattern so that a drowned sailor could be identified and returned to his home for burial.

The Aran Islands that lie off the west coast of Ireland have given their name to a unique knitting style made up of intricately interwoven Celtic cable patterns. They take inspiration from the ropes and chains of fishing boats and ancient Celtic symbols. Aran wool has traditionally been spun from the fleeces of the local sheep that survive the most inhospitable climate and bleak landscape by living on a diet of seaweed dragged ashore by the fishermen. Traditionally, Aran fishermen's sweaters were knitted in the undyed creamy white wool that was rich in oily lanolin, using patterns designed to maximize its insulating properties. Aran wool is now dyed in a broad range of colours and Aran is still one of the most popular and challenging knitting styles because of the variety of different stitches used for each garment.

The Shetland Islands lie off the north coast of Scotland. The islanders have a tradition of knitting square, fine lace shawls inspired by fine Spanish lace brought to the islands in the 16th century. It seems that the women of the Shetland Islands developed the particular skill of weaving especially fine yarns and would knit shawls five feet square that were fine enough to be pulled through a wedding ring. The wool was also exceptionally soft because the island sheep shed their fleeces naturally in the summer and could be plucked rather than shorn. This produced long strands with tapering ends. The knitted shawl patterns have an intricate look but are constructed from a combination of relatively simple stitches. The completed shawls are washed and pegged out on a frame to dry naturally, which 'sets' their square shape.

The colourful and patterned Fairisle knitting takes its name from another small Shetland island. Legend tells that a galleon from the Spanish Armada was wrecked off Fair Isle in the 16th century and sailors were washed up onto the shore wearing brilliantly coloured patterned knitted garments. Imagine the mixed emotions on the shore with the pity for the poor drowned sailor being overwhelmed by excitement over his fabulous jumper!

The islanders copied and reinterpreted the patterns and the name Fairisle is still synonymous with the knitting style. It is traditionally knitted in the round on four needles so that the right side is always facing outwards and only plain knit stitch is used on small areas of colour. The wool is simply carried across the back of the work and picked up again when needed. Originally, they dyed wool in muted shades using homemade vegetable dyes but when synthetic dyes became available in the early 20th century the patterns took on a new vibrancy. The islanders presented the then Duke of Windsor with a knitted sweater when he visited them in the 1920s and this unwitting product placement launched a Fairisle fashion when he was photographed wearing it to play a round of golf in the south of France.

The 'gansey' sweater knitted for and by the fishermen of Guernsey is the prototype for most of the fisherman's sweaters – or jerseys – whose name is derived from a different Channel island. They were knitted from dark blue dyed local wool that had a similar thickness to our double knitting but worked on much finer needles than we would use today. Sets of double-pointed needles or wires were used to knit the main body in the round creating a tight, water- and wind-repelling fabric. The women of Guernsey are known to have formed knitting cooperatives and traded to other fishing communities as long ago as the 16th century. Similar sweater styles existed in Cornwall and around the coast of Scotland.

There is an ancient tradition of knitting in Sweden, Norway and Finland where the winters are extremely cold and communities can be snowed in for many months of the year. The Scandinavians contrasted their snow white landscape with highly decorative homes and their everyday garments show their skill and love of pattern. They used distinctive motifs and often worked in starkly contrasting black and white. Dates and initials are often incorporated either knitted in or embroidered onto the knitted mittens, stockings and caps. Patterns such as reindeer, rose petals, people and chequerboards were the most popular in Norway. Cable stitching was another popular feature and fitted cardigans were made with geometrical bands of pattern around the neck, yolk and sleeves.

In Tunisia, shepherds have always knitted while tending their flocks. The product of their labours is the traditional red fez, which is knitted as a long tube then boiled up to make felt that is shaped on a block. Just like that!

Women famously knitted socks and Balaclavas to send to soldiers fighting in the First and Second World Wars. It meant far more to the soldiers than merely a way of keeping warm, as the knitting had been done by the soft hands of a woman back home. The knitting nurtured them and lifted their spirits. And, for the women, it provided a way to contribute and participate in the war effort even though they were far away from the Front.

In the 1950s and 1960s fashion favoured the new synthetic fabrics and home knitting fell from grace for a while. Then 'Earth Mothers' in fringed shawls knitted patchwork blankets to keep the hippies warm in the early 1970s and Fairlisle tank tops came back into vogue as *the* thing for a young man to be seen in when strutting his stuff in bellbottoms and a fitted velvet jacket. The last 'big' knitting revival was in the 1980s when huge batwing, padded-shouldered mohair creations were a fashion essential, along with very spiky hair and tight leggings. Motif knitting was all the rage, too, with anything from teddies to tigers adorning sweaters worn by young and old alike. The nature of fashion is that it changes and hand knitting kept a low profile during the minimalist nineties.

Knitting has staged a 21st-century comeback as a high-style craft activity. It's a worldwide phenomenon – championed by everyone from the anti-capitalist youth culture that venerates all things local, ethical and small scale to models and filmstars with money to buy anything their heart desires but a craving for the down-to-earth rarity of handmade fashion. Theories as to the origins of knitting's new wave of popularity abound, but, in the end, knitting is something that you cannot *pretend* to do. You either knit and enjoy it or you don't and no amount of paparazzi pictures of rock chicks knitting will make a knitter out of a quitter.

Handknitted clothes and home accessories have added value because they involve knitting for pleasure. We don't make sweaters, hats, gloves, warmers and throws from necessity anymore as these things are mostly cheaper to buy ready made. Cheaper perhaps, but not unique. We knit for the love of it and to make something ourselves to keep or to be given away with our love.

The rhythmic, repetitive activity of knitting has a calming effect and combats stress in the same way as yoga or meditation does, but with knitting you get something afterwards that you can hold in your hands.

Learning to knit gives us a chance to express our creative selves in colour and texture and, what's more, to do it more or less anywhere, anytime – while having a conversation, sunbathing, watching TV or travelling on a train.

One young knitting group in London meet up on the underground to knit, and groups all over the world are meeting on arranged 'knit nights' in cafés and bars to spend time together sharing their projects and stitches. Tap 'knitting' into any internet search engine and you will find a wealth of free patterns, advice, anecdotes and friendship. Knitters like to share.

Let's face it: knitting is pretty cool in the 21st century.

The downside is that it can be ever so slightly addictive.

How to use this book

Knitting patterns have traditionally been written with the assumption that everyone knows how to knit. On the contrary, many of us have been completely baffled by the complex instructions and abbreviations. This book will enable you to understand all the basics and read patterns with confidence.

The early pages familiarize you with the tools of the trade. The basics are a pair of needles and a ball of yarn but there are plenty of other bits and bobs that will come in useful.

Whether you buy yarn online or from a store, it comes in a bewildering range. The materials section of this Introduction shows some of the options and enables you to compare the relative scale of the most common categories, such as chunky, DK and 4 ply.

Chapters 2, 3 and 4 provide you with all the information you need to become a knitter: how to cast on and off; the basic knit and purl stitches; how to increase and decrease. The stitch samples, diagrams and illustrations provide a knitting reference section to refer back to any time you need to refresh your memory of what an instruction means or a particular pattern should look like.

All knitting is a variation of **knit** and **purl** and when you feel comfortable with the knit stitch you are ready to learn to purl. Once you get to grips with these two you will be on your way.

We all learn in different ways. If you prefer to perfect your technique before attempting a project then I suggest you knit sample squares, trying out the different stitches and techniques in a variety of yarns and needle sizes.

If you cannot wait to actually make something then move straight onto the first projects (in Chapter 5) and knit a scarf, a bag or a cushion cover.

All the projects in the book have been designed to be achievable for a new knitter. As each new type of stitch is introduced it is featured in a pattern, encouraging you to practise and apply what you have learned.

The level of complexity increases towards the end of book with the introduction of more advanced stitches and techniques such as cable and Fairisle. These projects are intended as an introduction to the techniques and as such have also been kept simple and achievable.

By the end of the book you will have gained the confidence to answer the question 'Can you knit?' with 'Yes, I can!' And knitting is a skill, like riding a bicycle, that once learned is never forgotten.

Knitting equipment

All you need in order to learn to knit is a ball of yarn and a pair of straight needles. The size of the needles and the weight of the wool you choose for your first attempt will make a big difference to both experience and results. Knitting needles come in a range of sizes from very fine 2mm that are used to knit fine lacy shawls to the very fat virtual broomsticks for super-chunky yarns.

Ideally, when you begin you need to use needles that are small enough to hold correctly and comfortably: 4–5mm are ideal. When you start off holding the needles in the correct position, your knitting style is destined to develop into an effortlessly smooth rhythm. I would recommend using a medium weight yarn, such as double knitting, to begin with. Your garment will take a while longer to grow than with chunky yarn, but knitting is as much about enjoying the activity as seeing the results.

Learn on big needles using chunky yarn and you will have to clutch the needles in your fists and lift your whole arm to move the yarn between the needles. The downside of this is you feel like a toddler – the upside is that fat needles and chunky yarns give quick results. If you are impatient or desperately need that scarf then this route will suit you best.

Knitting needles

Choose from plastic, aluminium or bamboo needles. We all prefer one sort to another and you need to knit with them to make your mind up. Needles are sold in a range of different sizes and lengths.

Plastic needles

These are lightweight and slightly bendy.

Buy high-quality named brands because cheaper needles have too much 'give' in them.

The small plastic needles do not suit heavyweight garments but the larger sized needles are tubular and very strong.

They come in a range of bright colours – especially the vintage needles that can be picked up cheaply secondhand. On the downside, the old ones were made of a more brittle material that can snap under pressure.

Aluminium needles

Aluminium is a very light, strong metal – ideal for making knitting needles. These needles will last a lifetime and make a pleasant clicking noise when you knit.

Old needles were made in a beautiful range of metallic colours but nowadays they tend to be coated with grey enamel. The neutral grey background has obviously been proved to give stitches most definition when knitting and counting.

Bamboo needles

Polished bamboo needles are gaining popularity among experienced knitters. It is a lightweight, strong and natural material that is a pleasure to hold in your hands. The only downside is that being made from a natural fibrous material the needles do occasionally have irregularities that cause them to split or splinter. When this happens they will shred the yarn. Nonetheless, they are a pleasure to use.

Cable needles

These are very short needles, sometimes with a dip in the middle, used when knitting cables. They are made in a range of sizes to match the thickness of the knitting needles.

Circular needles

A circular needle is two short needles joined by a length of nylon or plastic. They are made in the standard range of needle sizes and the length of the flexible section also varies to allow for different sized tubes to be knitted. They can also be used conventionally when knitting large items like blankets as the main weight of the knitting can lie in your lap instead of being carried on the needles.

Double-pointed needles

These are used in sets of four or five to knit tubular items such as socks. They are also used for Fairisle knitting patterns.

Needle gauge

Knitting needles used to be numbered differently in the UK from the rest of Europe but new needles are all metric now. The USA has a different system.

Refer to the chart for the full range.

A gauge is invaluable for checking the sizes of odd, old or foreign needles.

Stitch holders

These are made in a range of sizes and used to hold stitches that are not being knitted. When garments divide for a neckline, for instance, one half of the stitches are knitted while the other must wait their turn on a stitch holder.

Small numbers of stitches – such as the thumb of a glove – can be kept on safety pins but care should be taken as they can catch and shred the yarn.

Sewing needles

A wool supplier will have specialist needles for making up knitted garments. A tapestry needle or a darning needle can also be used. Choose one with a rounded end rather than a sharp point that can shred yarns.

Measuring equipment

A rule

A rigid clear plastic rule is the best tool for checking tension squares.

Tape measure

A small retractable tape measure is ideal for measuring your knitting.

Pins

Bright plastic-headed stainless steel pins are used when blocking and pressing garments before making up.

Scissors

A small pair of blunt-ended scissors will be needed to trim off yarn ends.

Knitting needles conversion chart			
	Continental (mm)	English	US
	$2\frac{1}{4}$	13	0
	$2\frac{3}{4}$	12	1
	3	11	2
	$3\frac{1}{4}$	10	3
	$3\frac{3}{4}$	9	4
	4	8	5
	$4\frac{1}{2}$	7	6
	5	6	7
	$5\frac{1}{2}$	5	8
	6	4	9
	$6\frac{1}{2}$	3	10
	7	2	$10\frac{1}{2}$
	$7\frac{1}{2}$	1	11
	$8\frac{1}{2}$	00	13
	9	000	15

Stitch and row counter

This is a small drum-shaped counter that slides up to the top of the needle shaft. It is twisted to move the numerals on and keep count of numbers of stitches.

Point protectors

Rubber or plastic stoppers go onto the needle ends when you are not knitting. These prevent the stitches from coming off the needles and will protect a knitting bag from being accidentally punctured.

Markers

These are small coloured rings used to mark the beginning of a row when knitting in the round on a set of double-pointed needles or a circular needle.

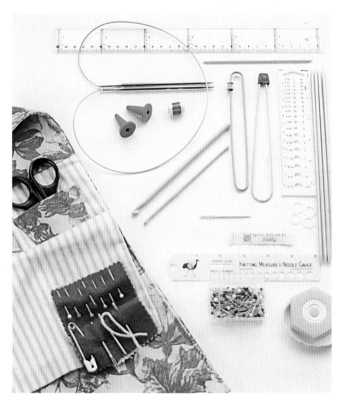

Materials

Knitting yarns come in many different weights and textures. They are manmade or natural or a mixture of the two.

Natural fleece yarns are manufactured from sheep wool, alpaca from llamas, cashmere and mohair from goats and angora from rabbits.

The natural plant yarns are cotton or linen made from flax or silk spun by silkworms that dine on mulberry leaves. Viscose and rayon have vaguely natural credentials as they are made from woodpulp that has to go through complex chemical processes to produce a yarn from cellulose.

Natural yarns are comfortable to wear next to the skin. Knitted cotton feels heavier than wool and is great for kids' garments as they often complain that wool is itchy.

Wool and cotton mixtures are a good compromise as they have all the best qualities of both yarns.

Mohair is soft and fluffy and feels quite glamorous. The wool is inclined to shed fibres. Mohair gives warmth without weight.

Angora is fluffy, too, but the shorter pile means it is less likely to shed. It is extremely feminine in character.

Silk has a surprisingly rough texture on its own and is exceptionally hard wearing. Fine spun and mixed with other yarns such as cashmere it becomes soft and luxurious.

Cashmere is simply the softest, warmest and lightest of all. Even 5% cashmere will make a noticeable difference to the feel of a yarn.

Synthetic or manmade yarns are never as warm as their natural equivalents but they have the big advantage of not shrinking, being easy to wash and dry and keeping their shape and colour. Children often prefer their feel.

Mixing a small percentage of synthetic yarn into cotton or wool can lend the yarn these same qualities without sacrificing its natural credentials.

Note: When buying yarn always check the dye lot number and make sure you buy enough for the whole project and that every ball has the same lot number. Yarn is placed into dye baths to colour it and the same shade can vary slightly even though it looks very similar. The fact that suppliers include a dye lot number shows that variations do occur.

Fancy yarns

Bouclé, chenille and metallic yarns have been around for a long time but the recent knitting boom has a lot to do with the invention of new fashion yarns such as eyelash, which knits up to look like fur, raggy yarn with knots and irregularities and cotton tape, which is broad and flat and is knitted on large needles to make airy summer garments and accessories.

Most familiar yarns

- 2, 3 and 4 ply – fine yarn, 2–3.5mm needles
- Sock wool – ultrafine yarn, 2–3mm needles
- Double-knitting (DK) – versatile medium weight easy knitting yarn, 4–5mm needles
- Chunky – about double the weight of DK, 6–8mm
- Super-chunky – double the weight of chunky size, 10–15mm needles.

02 the basics

In this chapter you will learn:

- how to hold the yarn
- how to hold the needles
- how to make the first stitch
- how to cast on
- how to knit various stitches
- about increasing
- about decreasing
- how to cast off
- knitting abbreviations
- how to follow a pattern
- how to measure
- how to knit a tension square.

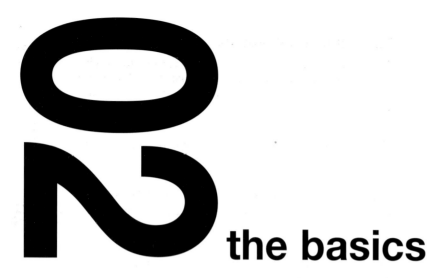

the basics

The basics

Being a beginner is always frustrating. You see the possibilities and want to progress as quickly as possible. A short time spent learning how to hold the needles and the wool at this stage will make you a much more efficient knitter for life.

It may seem uncomfortable at first but if you hold the needles and the wool properly your knitting will develop a rhythm and grow much faster. Once you have a confident rhythm going you will be able to relax and take your eye off the ball. Watch television, chat to friends, look at the scenery from a train or car window and all the while your knitting will be growing. One of the nicest things about knitting is that it is so portable and you can do other things at the same time.

Knitting know-how starts with a ball of wool and a pair of needles. I suggest you use short length size 5mm needles and a ball of double knitting wool as both are sturdy enough to be held comfortably and get swift results.

Holding the yarn

Looping the yarn around the fingers of your right hand creates a controlled tension for feeding the wool through to the needles as you knit. Mastering this will help you to produce neat, even tensioned knitting.

Weave the wool around your little finger (the pinkie) then under your ring and middle fingers and over your index finger. Use your pinkie to feed and adjust the tension of the wool. Persevere so that this comes naturally and your knitting will be faster, more even and more rhythmic because of it.

Note: These instructions are for **right-handed knitters**. If you are left-handed, I suggest you use a mirror to reflect the diagrams in reverse. Left-handers may not agree as most tend to find their own way of coping.

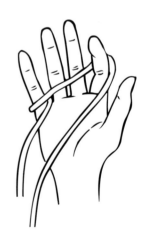

figure 2.1   Holding the yarn

Holding the needles
The English method

The English method is used to demonstrate the stitches in this book.

Hold the needle with the cast-on stitches in the palm of your left hand with your thumb across the stitches.

Keep the stitches 10–15cm from the needle point: too near the point you risk losing them; too far away you will need to stretch the yarn as you knit.

Wind the yarn around the fingers of your right hand as shown in Figure 2.1.

Hold the right needle between your thumb and index finger so that the needle lies on top of your hand following the line of your forearm.

Aim to knit with a taut 5cm length of wool between your needles and your index finger so that you minimize the movements you have to make as you knit.

The Continental method

This seems to suit those who have learned to crochet before they learned to knit and experts find it much faster. It also minimizes the movements you make when knitting.

Hold the needles with the cast-on stitches in your left hand.

Wind the yarn around the fingers of your left hand and twice around the index finger, keeping the ball of wool on the left.

The left hand is held still with the yarn tension created between the knitting, the index finger and the pinkie. The right hand holds the needle horizontally from above. The right needle is inserted through the stitch loop to draw the taut yarn through and make the new stitch while the knitted stitch is slipped off the needle. The new stitch remains on the right and further stitches are knitted until all the knitting is in the right hand.

The following row is started on the left once again.

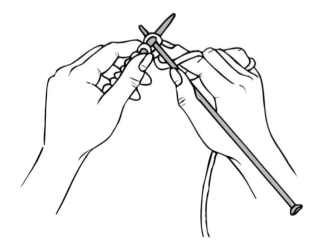

figure 2.2   Holding the needles – the English way

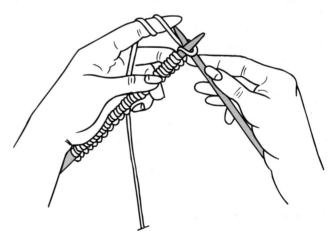

figure 2.3   Holding the needles – the Continental way

Making the first stitch

The first stitch on the needle is a slip knot.

Twist the yarn around your finger and pull a loop through and place it on the needle.

Pull the short end of the wool to tighten the knot so that it sits neatly on the needle.

It should be tight enough to slide easily along the needle but not so loose as to drop off the end.

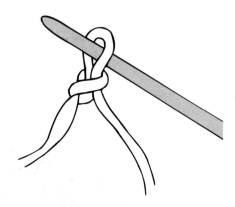

figure 2.4   Making the first stitch

Casting on
The two-needle method

Look at Figure 2.5.

1 Hold the needle with the first slip-knot stitch in your left hand. Hold the right-hand needle as if you were holding a pen with the wool feeding over between the knuckles of your right hand. Insert the right needle through the stitch on the left.

2 Wrap the yarn under the right needle.

3 Slide the needle back drawing the yarn through the stitch.

4 Now place this new stitch on the left needle above the first stitch.

You have now knitted your first cast-on stitch and can repeat this procedure to make as many stitches as you need.

Casting-on tips

1 Check that you keep the same tension as you cast on by pulling the yarn to firm up each stitch. Not too tight, though – remember you want a snug fit when you slide the other needle in to knit another cast-on stitch. If you have to force the needle into the loop it is too tight and if it drops out easily it is too loose.

2 It is worth being ruthless about the quality of your casting on. If your cast-on row looks uneven or too loopy then start again. You may be desperate to get on with your knitting but a bad edge can't be fixed later on and could spoil the look of the whole garment.

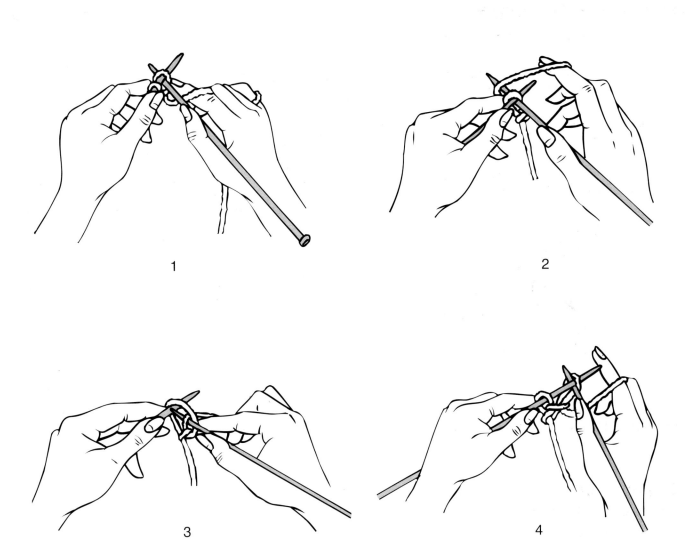

1

2

3

4

figure 2.5 Casting on with two needles

The thumb method

Stitches can be cast on using your left thumb and one needle held in the right hand as shown in Figure 2.6.

1 The first slip-knot stitch is made approximately 1m along the length of the yarn, although the length you need depends on the number of stitches being cast on. As a rough guide use 1m for every 100 stitches.

2 Holding the short end of the yarn in your left hand, wrap it round your thumb and keep its tension using your fingers against your palm.

3 Knit into the loop on your thumb using the yarn from the ball to make a stitch on the right needle.

4 Now make another loop on your thumb and knit into it to make a second stitch. When you have the right number of stitches turn and knit with the yarn from the ball in the usual way.

An edge made this way will be hard wearing with a nice stretchy quality.

There are several other variations in casting on and they produce different edges. If the stitches are made by knitting into the front of the stitch you create a looser edge, whereas knitting into the back makes the edge firmer. Stitches can also be made by not inserting the right needle into a stitch but into the space between two stitches.

Experiment to see which method suits you best.

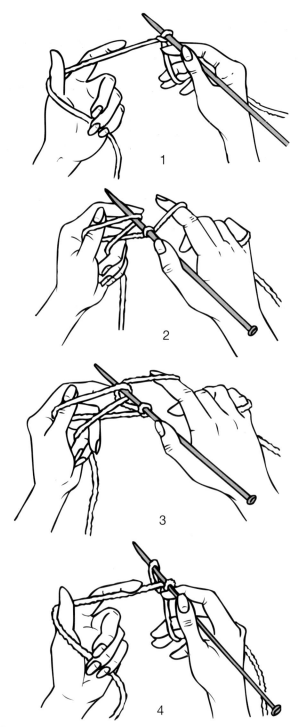

figure 2.6 The thumb method of casting on

Casting on with four needles

When you knit in the round using four double-pointed needles, the stitches are divided equally across three of them and the fourth is the working needle. In some countries, it is more common to knit in the round with five needles. This method is only suitable for knitting tubes, where it has two advantages: that there are no seams to be sewn and, for stocking stitch, that you only need to work in knit stitch not purl. Fairisle patterns with lots of colour changes are done this way.

Cast on using your usual method. There are two ways to divide the stitches:

1 Cast all the stitches onto one long needle then slip them onto three double-pointed needles.

2 Cast on the first third then introduce another needle next to it and cast on the next third and do the same again for the final third.

1

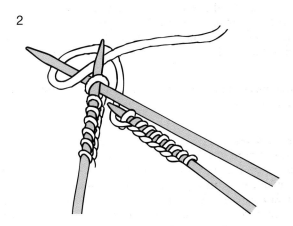

2

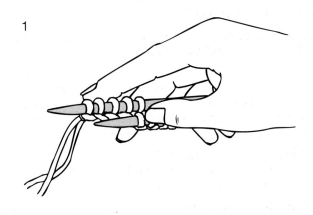

figure 2.7   Casting on with four needles

How to knit various stitches
Knit stitch

Also called plain stitch.

Hold the needle with the cast-on stitches in your left hand. Now look at Figure 2.8.

1 Insert the tip of the right needle through the first stitch from front to back. Take the yarn round the back and under the right needle then over between the needles. Raise your right index finger to keep the yarn's tension as you do this.

2 Retract the right needle, helping it with a little push from the tip of your left index finger. Dip the right needle under the stitch taking the loop of yarn with it. Slide the original stitch to the tip and drop it off the left needle.

3 You have knitted your first knit stitch!

Continue to the end of the row then turn the work, swap hands and do the same again.

Now cast on 10 stitches and knit 10 rows.

Cast off.

This is your first piece of knitting and is worth saving.

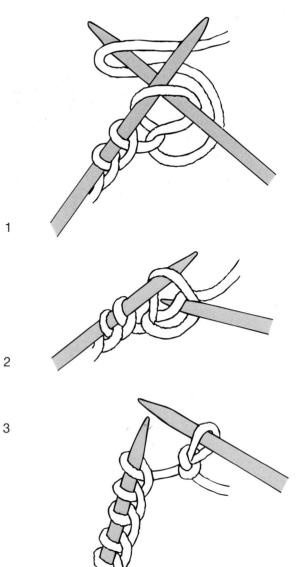

1

2

3

figure 2.8   Knit stitch

Purl stitch

Follow Figure 2.9.

1 Hold the needle with the cast-on stitches in your left hand and hold the yarn at the front of the right needle. Slide the tip of the right needle from right to left into the first stitch with the right needle in front of the left. Pass the yarn round the needle point.

2 Draw the loop through.

3 Keep the stitch on the right needle and allow the original stitch to drop off the left needle.

You have now knitted your first purl stitch.

Continue to the end of the row.

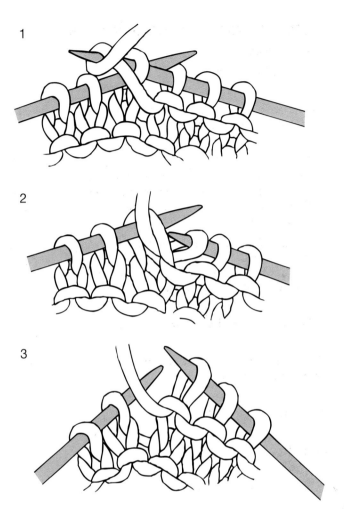

figure 2.9   Purl stitch

Garter stitch

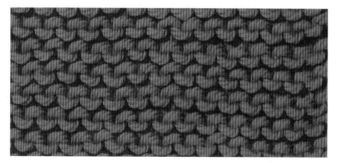

figure 2.10   Garter stitch

This can be worked on any number of stitches.

Row 1: k.

Garter stitch is made by using the knit or plain stitch just described to work every row. The effect is one of ridged wavy lines and it looks the same on both sides.

It stretches both ways and is the starting point for all knitters.

The same effect can be achieved by knitting all rows in purl stitch.

Garter stitch lies flat and is useful for creating borders.

Stocking stitch

This, too, can be worked on any number of stitches.

Row 1: k.

Row 2: p.

figure 2.11   Stocking stitch

Stocking stitch is made by knitting and purling alternate rows. One row knit is followed by one row purl to give a smooth surface on one side, usually the front, and a pebbled one on the back.

Reverse stocking stitch

Row 1: p.

Row 2: k.

Sometimes stocking stitch is worked the other way round and called reverse stocking stitch. This appears mostly in Aran knitting patterns where it creates more contrast between the cables, which are knitted in stocking stitch, and their background.

Twisted garter stitch

figure 2.12   Twisted garter stitch

Twisted garter stitch is done by knitting into the back of all the stitches. It has the same appearance as the usual method but the texture is much firmer.

Twisted stocking stitch

A twisted stitch is made by inserting the needle into the back of the stitch instead of the front. Doing this on the knit row of stocking stitch and working the purl row in the usual way produces a different, denser texture with a vertical zigzag effect. For a very minor variation, it creates a surprisingly noticeable difference.

Picking up a dropped stitch

This is bound to happen in the early stages so now is a good time to learn how to correct it.

The easiest way to do this is to use a crochet hook as it will catch the loop of the stitch and hold onto it as you weave the dropped stitch back up through the bars until it reaches the row you are working on.

A knit stitch appears at the front of the bar and a purl stitch behind it.

Unpicking mistakes

If you spot a mistake earlier in the row or the previous row do not despair. You need to work in reverse and unknit to the point of your mistake.

Hold the work in your right hand and insert the left needle into the row below. Transfer this stitch back onto the left needle and allow the top stitch to drop off. Keep doing this until you reach the mistake, rework it, then continue knitting.

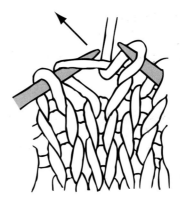

Unpicking – plain side

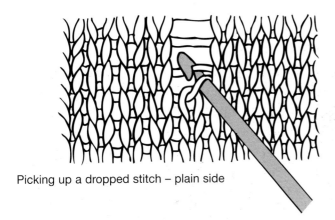

Picking up a dropped stitch – plain side

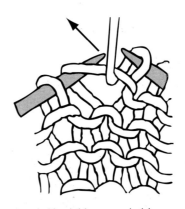

Unpicking – purl side

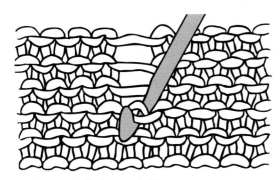

Picking up a dropped stitch – purl side

figure 2.13 Picking up a dropped stitch

figure 2.14 Unpicking – mistakes

Increasing

When knitting any shape other than a square or rectangle it is necessary to increase or decrease the number of stitches on the needle. If the stitches are increased or decreased on the outside edges it is called shaping, and when it is done within the row it is known as fashioning. There are several different ways to do this and each one gives a different visible decorative effect.

Increasing on the outside edge

The most basic shaping is done by casting on the required number of stitches by the thumb method at the beginning and end of the row.

figure 2.15   Increasing on the outside edge

Increasing on the inside edge

This is done within the row. Knit into the stitch in the usual way but before it is slipped off the left-hand needle bring the yarn forward and work a purl stitch into the same loop. This makes one extra stitch.

figure 2.16   Increasing on the inside edge

To create a symmetrical width increase, use this method on the third stitch from the beginning of the row and then again on the third stitch from the end of the row.

Pick-up increase (also called Make One)

This is done by picking up and knitting into the horizontal bar between the stitches from the previous row. The row is then continued in the usual way.

To create a symmetrical width increase pick up and knit into the bar after the second stitch from the start of the row and the bar before the second stitch from the end of the row.

Increase using 'overs'

This is the most obviously decorative method of increasing within the row.

Do this by wrapping the wool over the needle to create a new loop, which is worked as a stitch in the following row.

Symmetrical width increases by this method are done by forming the new loop after the third stitch has been worked at the start of the row and then doing the same before the third stitch from the end of the row. Using an 'over' creates a neat hole and a row of them will create an openwork pattern.

Double increases using 'overs'

These are done in the same way, by wrapping the yarn over the needle and knitting it as a stitch in the following row, except they are worked in pairs on each side of a central stitch within the row. They are most usually used to create pleats.

Decreasing

This reduces the number of stitches on the needle to make the work narrower. The simplest way to decrease is to knit two stitches together. The other method uses slipped stitches and is used for more decorative pattern work.

To give gradual shaping the decreasing is done on alternate rows and always on the plain row of stocking stitch.

When more than three stitches are to be decreased in succession, they are simply cast off at the start of the row.

Decreasing on the outside edge

Simple decreasing at the start of the outside edge is done by slipping the first stitch then knitting the second and passing the slipped stitch over it.

To decrease more than one stitch, slip the first, knit the next two or three together then pass the slipped stitch over.

If the edge is to be sewn up as a seam then the last two stitches in the row can simply be knitted together.

If a neater edge is required use this method instead: at the end of the row, do not work the last stitch but slip it onto the right-hand needle, turn the work and begin the next row by working the slipped stitch, slipping the next one, then passing the first stitch over it.

Single decreases within the row

Stitches decreased within the row and done by the slipped-stitch method create a decorative slanted pattern effect.

It is described in knitting patterns as sl1 k1 psso (slip one, knit one, pass slipped stitch over).

Symmetrical decreases

The decrease is worked in the purl row as sl1 p1 psso (slip one, purl one, pass slipped stitch over).

In a knit row, the decrease forms a slant to the left on the front of the knitting and on a purl row it forms a slant to the right on the front of the knitting.

Decreasing on the inside edge

When a sharper angle is required, more stitches are decreased at the ends of the rows.

To make a left-sloping decrease

Slip one, knit two together, pass slipped stitch over (sl1 k2tog psso).

To make a right-sloping decrease

Slip one knitwise, knit the second, then pass the slipped stitch over it. Then move the stitch back to the left needle and pass the next left stitch over it before moving it onto the right needle.

Be assured that these initially perplexing instructions will soon become familiar as they form the basis of all shaping and most decorative openwork patterns in knitting.

figure 2.17 Decreasing on the outside edge

figure 2.18 Decreasing on the inside edge

Casting off

Casting off is the secure way to finish a piece of knitting and prevent your work from unravelling. There are several different ways to do this, some more suited to one stitch than another. As a rule of thumb, casting off should always be done in the pattern you are using – this is especially important where a rib stitch is being worked as a border. Work the casting off following the same knit and purl sequence as your pattern and the cast off will keep the rib's stretchy quality. A plain knit cast-off row forms a fairly rigid chain that will restrict a garment's elasticity. It is important to relax your tension slightly when you cast off, as a tight edge will spoil the shape of your knitting.

Casting off 1

This is the most common way to cast off stitches. If you are working in rib, remember to keep knitting the plain and purl stitches for the cast-off row. See the diagram below.

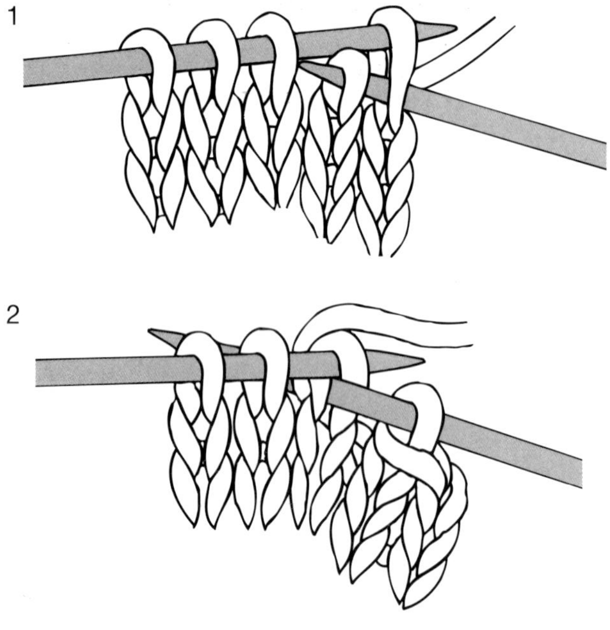

1 Work the first two stitches as usual then use the point of the left needle to lift the first stitch over the second and off the end of the needle.

2 Now, knit one more stitch and do the same again, working just one stitch each time until a single stitch remains.

Break the yarn and thread the end through this stitch and pull up firmly to secure it. The cast-off row will resemble a chain.

You can do this using a knit or purl stitch.

Casting off 2

This method makes a raised edge that had good elasticity.

It is especially useful for edges that are to be stitched together as seams.

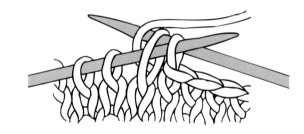

figure 2.20   Casting off 2

Knit two together (k2tog) through the back of the stitches. You will now have one stitch on the right needle. Slip it back onto the left needle and k2 tog with the next stitch, into the back of the stitches as before. Continue in this way until just one stitch remains, then break the yarn and thread the end through the loop and pull it up firmly.

figure 2.19   Casting off 1

Crochet casting off

A crochet hook of the same gauge as the needles is used to cast off in a chain stitch, which gives a neat, firm and decorative edge to the work. It can be worked in a contrasting colour to finish off a hat or a blanket.

1 Begin by using the crochet hook as you would the right knitting needle and knit the first two stitches from the left needle.

2 Now, use the crochet hook in its conventional way to draw the yarn through those two stitches.

3 You now have one new stitch on the crochet hook.

Knit the next stitch from the left needle onto the hook and once again draw the yarn through the two stitches.

Repeat this procedure until one stitch remains, then break the yarn and thread it though the loop and pull it up firmly.

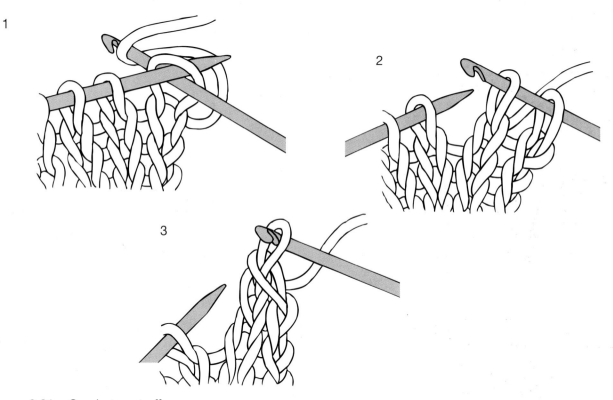

1

2

3

figure 2.21   Crochet cast off

Knitting abbreviations

If you are unfamiliar with knitting abbreviations, they can be extremely offputting. Patterns can resemble complex mathematical equations at a first and even a second glance. Abbreviations were introduced to compress long patterns but in doing so it seemed a whole new language had to be invented.

I hope that this book will help give you the confidence to unravel the mystery and to understand knitting patterns.

The important thing to remember is that all knitting is basically plain and purl with stitches added or taken away at regular intervals to produce the textured patterns:

**	the section between asterisks is to be repeated
alt	alternate
approx	approximate
beg	beginning
cc	contrasting colour
cm	centimetre
cont	continue
dec	decrease
foll	following
g st	garter stitch
grm	gram
in	inch
inc	increase
k	knit
kb	knit into the back of the stitch
k1 b	knit into the stitch below the next stitch then let them both drop off the left needle together
k2tog	knit two together to decrease
k up	pick up and knit
k-wise	knitwise – as you would make a knit stitch
LH	left hand
m1	make one – increase by knitting into both front and back of next stitch

mc	main colour
mm	millimetre
No	number
patt	pattern
psso	pass slipped stitch over
p	purl
p up	pick up and purl
p-wise	purlwise – as you would make a purl stitch
rem	remaining
rep	repeat
rnd	round
RH	right hand
Rs	right side facing
sl	slip
sl st	slip a stitch without knitting it
st st	stocking stitch
tbl	through the back of the loop
tog	together
Ws	wrong side facing

It may take a bit of time to fathom the following yrns and yons but they are the ones used to make neat holes for lacework or eyelets:

ybk	yarn back between needles
yfwd	yarn forward between needles
yon	yarn over needle
yrn	yarn round needle

Cable abbreviations

The number of stitches will vary according to the pattern:

cN	cable needle
c4B	slip 4 stitches onto a cable needle and keep them at the back
c4F	slip 4 stitches onto a cable needle and keep them at the front

How to follow a pattern

Knitting patterns are set out in a standard way. The key ingredients at the start of the pattern are **sizing, yarn requirements, needle size, tension** and **abbreviations.**

The pattern has been designed to fit an average size for an adult or an average aged child. This measurement will appear first in the pattern followed by another square-bracketed series of numbers referring to gradual increases in size.

For example:

> **Child's sweater**
>
> **Age** 2 [4: 6: 8: 10]
>
> **To fit chest** 56cm [61: 66: 71: 76]
>
> **Double knitting wool** Number of balls required 6 [6: 7: 7: 8]
>
> **Needles** 1 pair 4mm, 1 pair 3.75 mm
>
> **Tension** 22 stitches and 28 rows per 10cm square
>
> **Abbreviations used** alt = alternate; beg = beginning; cont = continue; k = knit; p = purl

The pattern will then be set out in sections such as front, back, sleeves.

Asterisks show what section of the row is to be repeated.

For example:

> Using 4mm needles cast on 68 [74: 84: 90: 96] stitches
>
> Row 1: k1 *p2 k2* to last stitch, k1.

This means you are beginning and ending the row with a knit stitch but in between you are working a rib stitch.

Round brackets are used to show pattern instructions that are to be repeated and the brackets will be followed by a number.

For example:

> (yfwd, sl1, k1 psso) x2

This means: Bring the yarn to the front, slip one stitch onto the right needle without knitting it, knit one stitch then use the left needle to lift the slipped stitch over the last knit stitch and then off the needle. The brackets and number denotes that this sequence must be followed twice.

You can now see why abbreviations are necessary!

How to measure

Pattern dimensions will be listed but it is also a good idea to take the measurements of the lucky person you are knitting for – and that includes yourself.

Measure these key areas:

> **Chest:** straight across the back under the arms and across the fullest part of the chest.
>
> **Shoulder:** from the tip of the shoulder to the base of the neck.
>
> **Neck:** around the neck at collar level.
>
> **Armhole depth:** from top of shoulder to 2.5cm below the armhole.
>
> **Underarm to waist:** from 2.5cm below armpit to natural waistline.
>
> **Hip:** around the fullest part of the hips.
>
> **Arm:** around the fullest part of the upper arm.
>
> **Sleeve length:** from 2.5cm below armpit to the inside wrist.
>
> **Wrist:** around the arm just above the wrist bone.

If you need to make any adjustments, you can refer to the tension. This tells you how many stitches there will be per 10cm and how many rows are worked to give a depth of 10cm when using the suggested yarn and needles.

For example:

A pattern has been designed to fit an 80cm bust and has 120 stitches per row. The tension measurement gives a width of 20 stitches per 10cm.

This tells you that, to make the garment fit an 85cm bust you will need to add another 10 stitches, so you cast on 130 stitches.

The same pattern gives the sleeve measurement as 44cm. The tension measurement gives a depth of 28 rows per 10cm.

This tells you that to shorten the sleeve length by 4cm you would need to work 7 fewer rows than the pattern suggests. (Note: this will only be relevant if you are using a pattern such as cable or Aran, where certain numbers of rows make up the design. If the sleeves are shaped with increases or decreases then it is best to add or take off length in a straight section where these do not occur.)

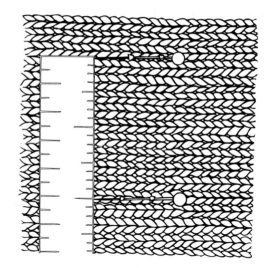

figure 2.22   Counting stitches

The tension square

Most beginners are impatient to begin and it is difficult to persuade them to knit a 10cm square before the main event. However, it is important – it makes you a better knitter and it makes sure you don't spend weeks knitting something that doesn't fit.

To make a tension square follow the guidelines in the pattern for knitting a 10cm square. Cast on the stated number of stitches and knit the stated number of rows. Now pin your square out flat and use a rule to take measurements. If your square measures 10cm × 10cm you will be able to follow the pattern exactly as it has been written. If not, there are adjustments to be made.

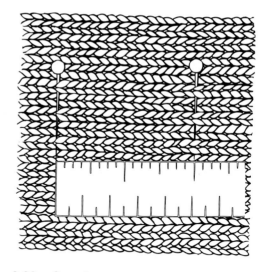

figure 2.23   Counting rows

The width or horizontal tension is the most important one to get right as the length can be adjusted by knitting fewer or more rows.

Changing needle size

The size of the needles used with the same yarn will change the size of the sample quite dramatically. The examples show three yarn weights knitted on fine 2mm needles and again on large 6mm needles.

- If your tension sample has more stitches than the stated number per 10cm, try knitting another sample on needles that are one size larger.
- If you have fewer stitches than the stated number, then try knitting another sample on needles that are one size smaller.

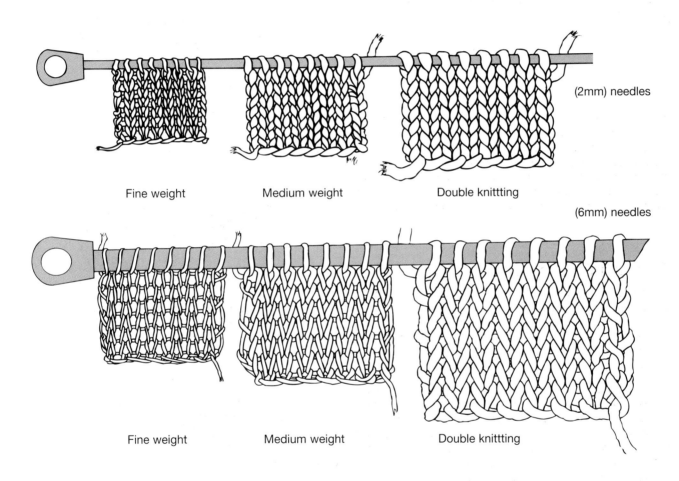

(2mm) needles

Fine weight   Medium weight   Double knittting

(6mm) needles

Fine weight   Medium weight   Double knittting

figure 2.24   Changing needle size

03 details

In this chapter you will learn:

- about side selvedges and borders
- how to knit a hem
- how to make buttonholes
- about knitting in the round
- about making up, blocking and pressing
- how to fit a zip
- how to add a ribbon facing
- how to make cords, pompoms, tassels and fringes.

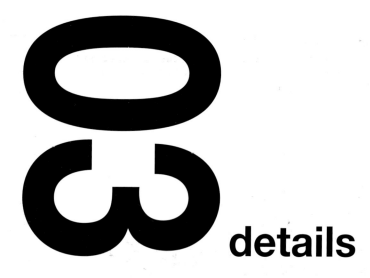

details

Side selvedges and borders

These will give your work a finished appearance and also make it easier to sew up nice flat seams.

Selvedges

A selvedge is a narrow border worked on the outside edge of a piece of knitting. Its purpose is to give the knitting a neat and regular edge. This is done by adding two stitches when casting on if the edge is to be sewn as a seam. They are worked in the same way at the start and end of every row, regardless of the other pattern details.

A wider band is made by working two stitches in the same way at the start and end of each row. This gives a more pronounced decorative effect and it will also prevent stocking stitch from curling up at the edges.

Slipped chain edge

This is used with garter stitch where the edges are to be sewn together as a seam or when stitches are to be picked up and knitted as a border. The terms 'knitwise' and 'purlwise' explain the direction to insert the needle when you slip a stitch.

Hold the yarn at the front of the work and slip the first stitch in every row purlwise, then take the yarn to the back and knit in the usual way.

figure 3.1   Slipped chain edge

Single garter stitch edge

This provides a firm edge for stocking stitch or for an openwork pattern where edges can be loose. Also use this one where seams are going to backstitched.

Knit the first and last stitches of every row.

figure 3.2   Slipped garter edge

Borders

These can be either be incorporated into the main body of the knitting by working a band of garter or moss stitch along the pattern edge or by picking up stitches from the selvedge edge and knitting a border. They can also be worked as separate button bands to be sewn on when the garment is made up.

Picking up stitches to knit

This is the neatest way to add collars, cuffs or an edging band without the tedious business of knitting a narrow band and sewing it on later.

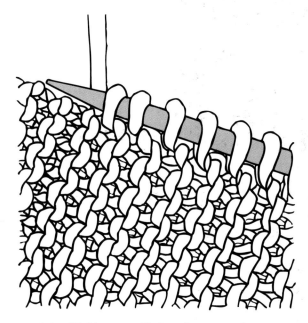

figure 3.3   Picking up stitches from an edge

Divide the edge into equal sections, marking their position with pins. This will enable you to pick up evenly along the edge.

Hold the work in your left hand with the right side facing and a needle in your right hand. Insert the needle under the edge stitch and knit the first stitch.

You now have one stitch on the right needle. Continue this way, picking up and knitting an equal number of stitches from each section you have marked. The first row will be knitted on the wrong side.

A crochet hook can also be used. Hold the work right side facing and insert the hook under the first stitch to pick up the yarn and draw it through to the front. Transfer it onto a knitting needle and pull up tight. Repeat this to the end. The first row is knitted on the right side.

Garter stitch border

To make the border firmer, knit into the back of the stitch to make a twisted garter stitch.

Knit every row then cast off.

figure 3.4   Garter stitch border

Moss stitch border

This gives a nice firm and decorative border.

Moss stitch is worked on an even number of stitches:

Row 1: *k1 p1*. Repeat to the end of the row.

Row 2: *p1 k1*. Repeat to the end of the row.

figure 3.5   Moss stitch border

Crochet borders

A crochet border creates a pretty edge that can be worked in a contrasting colour for added decorative effect. As a knitter, I find crochet difficult to begin from scratch as it lacks the solid base of a pair of needles. Borders are a lot easier, because you have the knitted piece as your base for your crochet.

Simple crochet border

Insert the hook into the first stitch, yarn over the hook at the back of the work and draw the loop through making one stitch on the hook; yarn over hook making another stitch; yarn over hook and draw through both stitches. Repeat to the end.

The following row is worked through the spaces of the first row.

figure 3.6   Crochet border

Knitting hems
Knitting a picot hem
Method 1
Worked at the end of the knitting:

figure 3.7 Picot hem – method 1

At the beginning of the row, cast on an extra two stitches.

Cast off these two stitches knitting into them as you would in a normal cast off.

Cast off one or two or more stitches in the normal way depending on the gaps you want between the picots.

Return the remaining stitch on the right needle to the left needle and cast on two stitches.

Cast off these two stitches and repeat to the end of the row.

Method 2
Worked at the beginning of the knitting:

figure 3.8 Picot hem – method 2

Cast on and work 2.5cm in stocking stitch.

Make an even spaced number of eyelet holes across the knitting like this: *k3, yrn, k2 tog*. Repeat to the end of the row.

Purl the following row in the usual way and you will have made a series of neat round holes. To finish off, fold up a hem along the middle of the row of holes and slip stitch the hem in place.

Knitting a plain hem

Sometimes a garment needs a thicker, more hard-wearing hem and this method will give you that and make a crisp edge at the same time.

Cast on loosely and work in stocking stitch until you have reached the depth you want for your hem, finishing on a purl row. Work the next row in purl to make a ridge on the right side of the work. This will be the fold line of your hem and you should start measuring the garment length from this point.

Blending the hem into the garment
When you have worked to the same depth as the hem, at the end of a knit row, fold the hem up and pick up and purl a stitch from the cast-on edge with each stitch from the left needle.

Alternatively, finish off the hem by turning it up and using the same wool to slip stitch it to the back of the work, as shown in Figure 3.9.

figure 3.9 Blending the hem

Buttonholes
Eyelet buttonholes

These are most usually used for baby clothes. They are small, neat round holes made by wrapping the yarn round the needle (yrn), then knitting the following two stitches together (k2tog). See Figure 3.11 for more explanation of thr two manoevres. The following row is worked as normal.

figure 3.10   Eyelet button holes

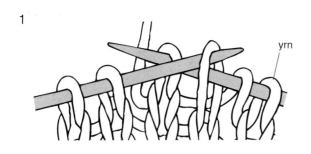

1

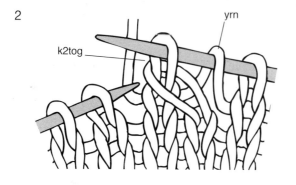

2

k2tog

yrn

figure 3.11   Yrn and k2tog

Horizontal buttonholes
Method 1

figure 3.12   A horizontal button hole

Knit to the point where the buttonhole is required.

Right side: Cast off the number of stitches needed for the buttonhole opening.

Wrong side: Knit to within one stitch of the opening and increase by working into the front and back of this stitch. Now cast on one stitch fewer than the number cast off.

Continue the row and the buttonhole will have been made.

figure 3.13   A neater horizontal button hole

Method 2

There is a far neater method worked in a single row. When knitted on garter stitch and reverse stocking stitch it is virtually invisible, and in stocking stitch it still gives a neater result. It looks complex but as soon as you have done it once, everything becomes clear. It is well worth learning!

Knit along the row to the point where the buttonhole is required.

Bring the yarn to the front (yfd) and slip the next stitch from the left to the right needle (s1).

Take the yarn around the back and leave it there (yb).

Working without the yarn, slip the next stitch from the left to the right needle then pass the first slipped stitch back over it (psso).

This sequence * – * is repeated until you have the width of buttonhole you require.

Slip the last stitch on the right needle back onto the left then turn the work to the other side.

Pick up the yarn and cast on the number of stitches you cast off plus one extra using the two needle cast-on method.

Before you slip the last cast-on stitch onto the left needle, bring the yarn to the front between the needles.

Turn the work round to face the front again.

Slip the first stitch from the left needle onto the right, pass the extra cast-on stitch over it and return the yarn to the back of the work.

This completes the buttonhole.

Vertical buttonholes

These are made by turning and working the two sides of the opening separately.

figure 3.14   A vertical buttonhole

Knit to the point where the buttonhole opening is required.

Move the stitches that remain on the left needle onto a stitch holder.

Turn the work and knit several rows using the remaining stitches.

When your buttonhole is deep enough, finish at the edge of the work and break the yarn.

Place this section on a stitch holder or safety pin until you need the stitches again.

Transfer the stitches that are being rested on the stitch holder back onto a needle and work with them until the two sides are the same depth.

Replace the stitches from the holder onto the needle.

Finish the buttonhole by knitting a wrong side row across both sections to rejoin them as a single row.

Knitting in the round

When you need to knit a tube, it is often easier to do it on a set of four double-pointed needles or a circular needle.

Knitting on four needles

Starting off is the most awkward part.

Cast the stitches onto a single needle first, then divide them equally between three needles. Alternatively, cast a third onto one needle then move to a second needle and then a third, casting an equal number of stitches onto each one.

Form the needles into a triangle with the first and last stitch adjacent. Make sure that none of the cast-on edges has become twisted on the needles.

Knit the first stitch keeping the yarn as tight as possible then continue to knit until all the first needle's stitches have been transferred to the fourth needle. Keep working around the needles in this way.

When several rows have been worked the whole operation becomes a lot easier as it is amalgamated into a single item instead of lots of different spiky ones!

Once you have mastered holding four needles instead of two, you will discover the advantages.

One is that your work is seamless and the other is that all rows are worked on the right side in plain knit stitch but the effect is one of stocking stitch. Fairisle is usually done this way with the different coloured yarns being stranded across on the inside of the knitting.

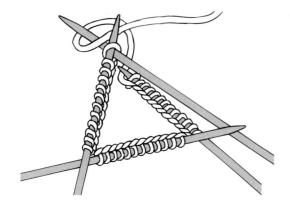

figure 3.15   Knitting on four needles

Garter stitch is worked as continuous purl – so the reverse to the usual applies.

To work rib in the round you should begin with a knit stitch and end with a purl stitch and groups of stitches should not be worked across the change from one needle to another.

Circular needles

These are actually short rigid plastic or metal needles joined together with a length of bendable plastic. The needles come in a range of five length sizes, from 40cm to 100cm, and in the usual range of needle width sizes.

They are used to knit garments in the round and their only limitation is that the garment has to have a 40cm or wider circumference; anything smaller will need to stretch to meet up and will be better suited to knitting on a set of four needles. Examples of this would be gloves, socks and baby leggings.

To knit a tube cast on the required number of stitches. Hold the needle with the last cast-on stitch on the right and join the circle by knitting into the first cast-off stitch on the left needle. Keep the yarn taut, as shown in Figure 3.16, as you bridge the gap and the join will not be obvious. All rounds are worked as knit but appear as stocking stitch on the outside of the tube. To knit garter stitch all rows must be worked as purl.

Circular needles can be used in the conventional way as shown in Figure 3.17 (knitting then turning at the end of the row). When knitting very wide garments such as bedspreads, the plastic wire can hold about four times the number of stitches that a rigid needle would. It also allows the weight of the knitting to rest in your lap instead of being supported on the needles. This is something you will only really appreciate when you take on a large project, such as a throw.

Using markers

When you knit in the round, it is sometimes difficult to see where the rounds begin and this is, of course, important when you come to count them. The simplest way to keep track is to place a coloured marker in front of the first stitch and move it up the work as you knit. If you are knitting the body of a sweater it is also useful to place a marker at the halfway point so that you can distinguish the 'front' from the 'back' of the work.

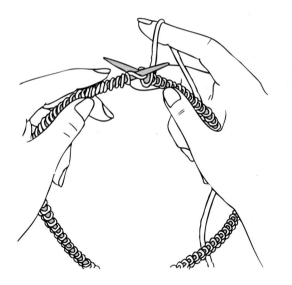

figure 3.16   Using circular needles to knit in the round

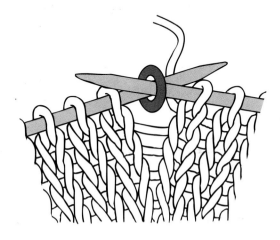

figure 3.18   Using a marker

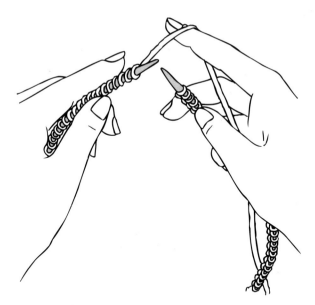

figure 3.17   Using circular needles for conventional knitting

Making up, blocking and pressing
Sewing up seams

Sewing up edge-to-edge seams

This is the method to use for lightweight garments as it forms no ridge and if done carefully, it will be virtually invisible.

Lie the two sections face down, side by side so that the rows and stitches are aligned.

Thread a tapestry needle and, using a single strand of matching yarn, sew though loops of opposite stitches alternately.

Do not pull the yarn too tight as it will lose its elasticity.

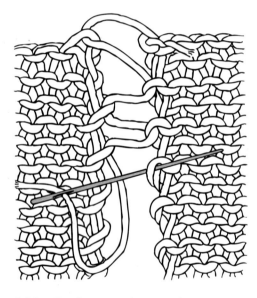

figure 3.19 Sewing up edge-to-edge seams

Backstitching side seams

This method is better for chunkier garments, rib stitch and where you have added a special selvedge edge that is different from the main body of the garment pattern. This is most similar to the seams you make when working with fabrics.

Place the two pieces together with their right sides facing.

Align the rows and the stitches.

Thread the needle with a single strand of matching yarn and sew through the centre of adjacent stitches, taking the needle back to complete the stitch then a matching length forward to make a new stitch.

Keep the stitches the same size and do not pull the yarn too tight.

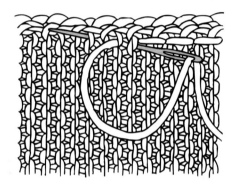

figure 3.20 Backstitching seams

Joining seams with a three-needle knitted cast off

This is a very neat way to finish off shoulder seams. You need three needles of the same size – one for the back, one for the front and one to knit with.

Once the front and back sections have been completed do not cast off. Instead keep the stitches on the needle – a stitch holder can be used until you are ready to knit the edges together.

Place the back and front sections together with wrong sides facing each other.

Line up the needles holding the two sections in your left hand with the needle points facing the same way.

Use the spare needle in your right hand to knit through a stitch from both needles at the same time.

Cast off in the usual way until you have one stitch left on each needle, then break the yarn, thread through and pull to make a secure knot.

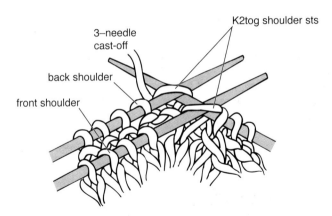

figure 3.21   Joining seams with a knitted cast off

Blocking

Knitted garments all benefit from being given this treatment before they are sewn up. It does not take a great deal of time and it will make the assembling all the easier if every piece has been blocked. Be sure to use stainless steel pins as other metals may leave rust marks:

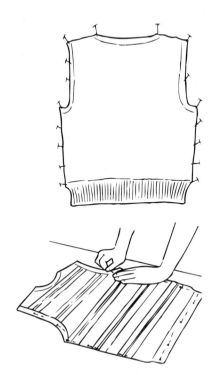

figure 3.22   Blocking

- Cover a tabletop with a thick towel or a blanket topped with a sheet.
- Place the pieces face down on the sheet.
- Check the measurements given for each piece in the pattern.
- Pin the pieces down to match those measurements making sure that the rows run in straight lines.
- Rib should be stretched lightly widthways to open it out slightly.

Pressing

After blocking, the garment is dampened and pressed to 'fix' the shape. This can be done by spraying with a mist of clean water and leaving it to dry naturally, but using a steam iron or a warm iron and a damp cloth is quicker and more effective.

- Place the damp cloth on the knitting and press the iron directly, but lightly, down onto it.
- Do not exert any real pressure as this will spoil the texture of the knitting.
- Do not move the iron as you do for normal ironing.
- Lift and press repeatedly until you have covered all the pieces.
- Do not remove any of the pins until the work is bone dry.

figure 3.23   Pressing

figure 3.24   Pin the zip first *(opposite)*

45

details

03

Fitting a zip

Wherever possible, it is a good idea to fit a zip before sewing up the rest of the garment. This way the edges will be more accessible and easier to stitch:

- Place the closed zip right side up on a flat surface.

- Place one side of the knitting, also right side up, along the tape of the zip.

- Pin the knitting to the zip, as shown in Figure 3.24, being careful not to stretch it out of shape.

- Pin the other side of the garment to the zip in the same way, making sure that the rows match and one end is not longer than the other.

- Check that the zip opens and closes easily and that the teeth are clear of the knitted edge.

- Tack the zip in place using smallish stitches and a contrasting colour thread – see Figure 3.25.

- Sew by hand using polyester thread in a matching colour, working in a small backstitch along the middle of each side of the zip tape. This is also shown in Figure 3.25.

- Oversew the ends several times as this is where most of the stress will be.

- Pull out the tacking stitches and press with a warm iron and a damp cloth.

- An open-ended zip should also be fitted closed to ensure that the zip is properly aligned.

figure 3.25   Tack then sew the zip

Adding a ribbon facing

A ribbon facing will prevent a buttoned edge from pulling out of shape and stop buttonholes from stretching.

A sewing machine will make the neatest buttonholes but they can also be sewn by hand:

- Cut two lengths of tape or ribbon to fit along the edges of the garment.

- Slipstitch the one that will hold the buttons in place.

- Tack the second length to the other edge and mark the positions for the buttonholes.

- Remove the tape and oversew the buttonholes either by hand or machine.

- Pin it to the garment making sure that the sewn and knitted buttonholes are aligned.

- Now slipstitch the second tape to the garment.

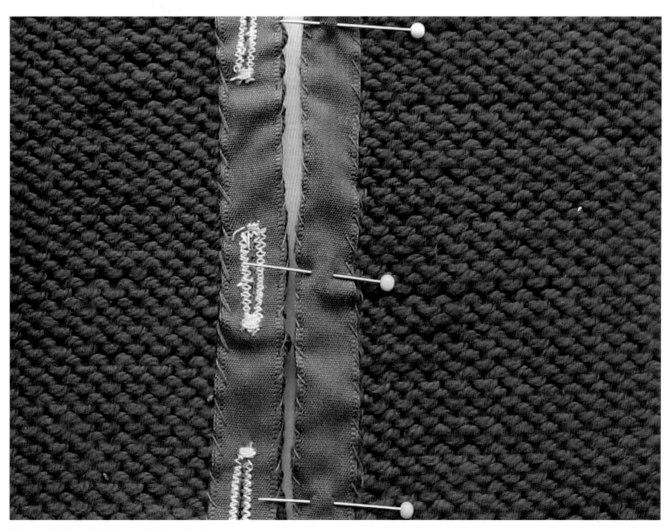

figure 3.26   Adding a ribbon facing

Making cords, pompoms, tassels and fringes

Twisted cord

As with the pompom there is a touch of magic or even theatre about making a twisted cord. You follow a procedure and then it suddenly takes on a life of its own and the result is a very smart twisted cord. Voilà!

> **Materials**
> Yarn four times the length of the cord you want to make
> A drawing pin and a firm surface

Making the cord

- Fold the cord in half and fasten the folded end to a surface with the drawing pin.
- Roll the other two thread ends together in the same direction until they twist together and begin to curl up.
- Keeping the twisted yarn taut, fold it firmly in half and join the end you are holding to the pinned end. The cord will twist and wind around itself.
- Fasten the ends with a knot.
- This is where you take the applause. Bravo!

figure 3.27　Making a twisted cord

Plaited cord

Cut three equal lengths of yarn.

Tie a knot at one end and pin to a surface.

Plait the ends tightly or loosely, as you prefer, and tie another knot at the end.

figure 3.28　Making a plaited cord

Pompoms

There is something rather magical about making pompoms. They look nothing special until you cut through the outer edge and tie them, then suddenly they emerge like fluffy day-old chicks! Teach a child how to make a pompom and he will want to make another 10 straightaway.

Materials

Two circles of cardboard of the pompom size plus another 2cm

A pair of sharp scissors

A tapestry needle

Several 2m lengths of yarn

Making the pompom

- Cut holes in the middle of the card about one-fifth of the size to make two wide rings.

- Thread the yarn onto the needle and use it double.

- Hold the two rings together and wind the yarn evenly around them until the hole in the middle is filled in.

- Hold firmly and insert the point of the scissors at the edge between the two pieces of card and cut through the yarn at the outside edge.

- Pull the two circles just slightly apart and tie a piece of yarn tightly between them, keeping these ends long enough to use for attaching the pompom.

- Cut the card away and remove it.

- Fluff up the pompom and trim it to make a nice round shape.

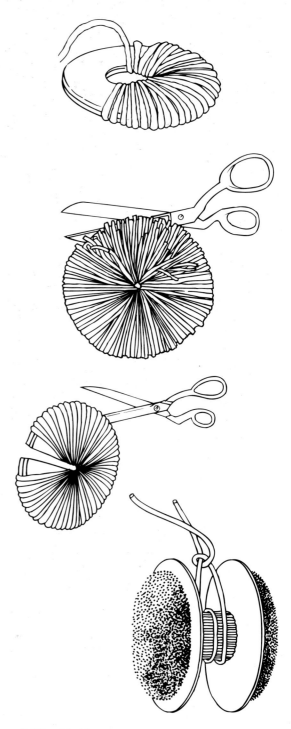

figure 3.29　Making a pompom

Tassels

A tassel is a nice way to finish off a hat or to make a decorative zip pull.

They can be made in any length and be as fine or chunky as you like.

Materials

A square of cardboard of the required tassel size

A piece of yarn to match the length and width you would like the tassel to be

A pair of scissors

A tapestry needle

Making the tassel

- Wind the yarn around the card to get the thickness you want.

- Thread the needle with a length of matching yarn and slip it under the loops at one end of the card and tie a knot to hold all the loops together.

- Remove the card and wind the yarn neatly around the top quarter of the tassel length then take the thread up through the middle and out the top.

- Hold the tassel in one hand and cut through the looped ends and trim into shape.

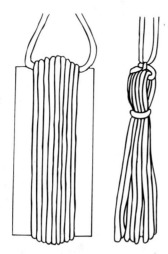

figure 3.30   Making a tassel

Fringes

Fringes add decorative flourish to the edges of scarves, bags and shawls. They can also be used in many other ways on garments or accessories.

Materials

Strands of yarn cut twice the length you want the fringe to be

A crochet hook

A tape measure

Pins

Sharp scissors

Making the fringe

- Measure the length to be fringed and divide it into equal sections marked with pins. Decide on the number of tassels per section.

- Fold the strands in half and use the crochet hook to pull the folded loops through to the other side of the knitting along the cast-off row.

- Now draw the long strands through this loop and pull up tightly to the top.

- Repeat along the edge making the same number of tassels per section and always working from the same side.

- Trim the fringe with sharp scissors.

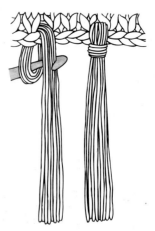

figure 3.31   Making a fringe

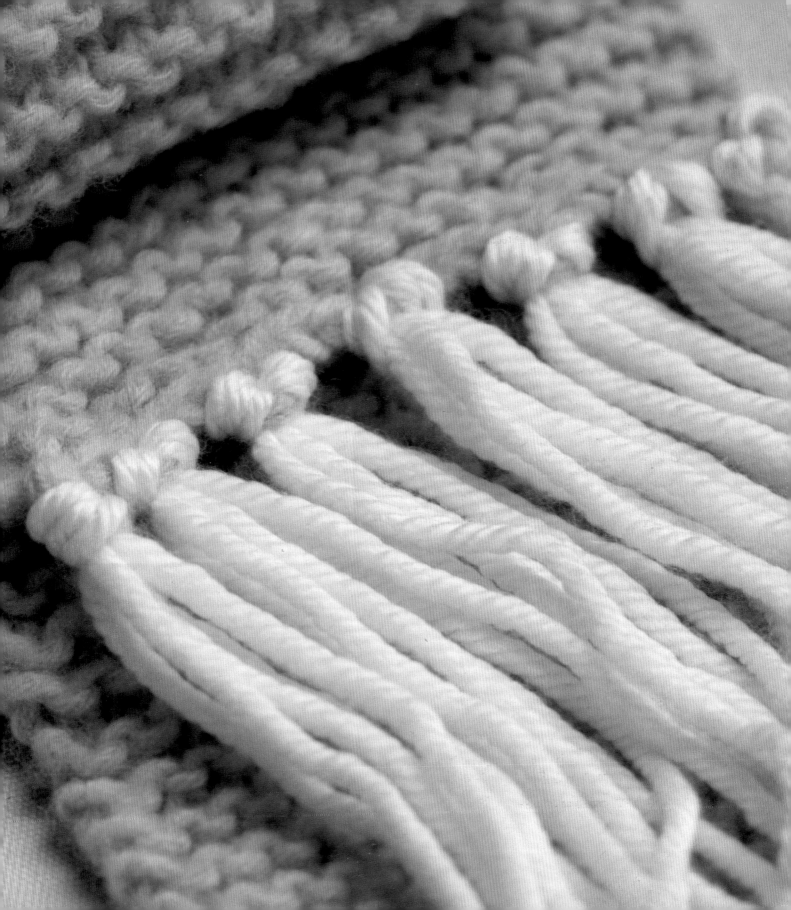

04 stitches

In this chapter you will learn:

- about rib stitches
- about moss stitches
- about textured patterns
- about cable stitch
- about openwork stitches
- how to make motifs and letters.

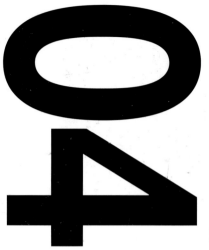

stitches

Rib stitches

Ribbing is worked by alternating sets of knit and purl stitches. This gives the work elasticity, and 20 single rib stitches will appear half the width of 20 worked in stocking stitch. The rib can be stretched widthwise to match the stocking stitch but it will spring back on release. Traditionally, jumpers have a ribbed neck opening, cuffs and welt, which is a term used to describe the band at the lower edge on the waist or hip.

There are also plenty of distinctive ribbing styles that are used as whole garment patterns in their own right. The single and double rib are explained now and the same method can be applied to knitting a triple or quadruple rib, by increasing the number of stitches in each set. The English or fisherman's rib is very popular for its warm insulating quality, and a single or double rib gives a snug body-hugging fit to skinny-rib jumpers. Children prefer ribbed jumpers because their stretchiness allows for plenty of movement and they can grow with the child, so they last longer as well.

Single rib

This is the simplest rib stitch and has the appearance of vertical lines of knit stitches. The purl stitches are set back and revealed when the work is stretched widthways. The work is identical on both sides.

Single rib can be worked on an odd or even number of stitches in straight knitting but only on an even number in circular knitting where the same stitches are knitted and purled for every round.

It is done by working a knit and purl stitch alternately to the end of the row.

On the following row, the order reverses so you work a purl stitch first.

Row 1: k1 p1.

Row 2: p1 k1.

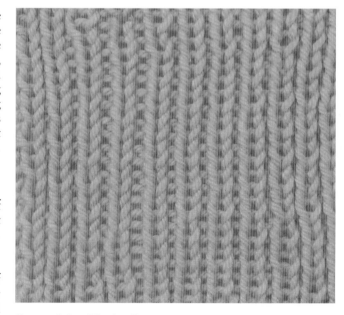

figure 4.1   Single rib

Double rib

This style of rib forms broader vertical stripes of raised plain and set back purl stitches. The work is identical on both sides.

It is worked by knitting two stitches then purling two stitches to the end of the row. On the following row, the order reverses and the first two stitches are purled.

In circular knitting, the same stitches are knitted and purled in every round.

Row 1: k2 p2.

Row 2: p2 k2.

figure 4.2   Double rib

Reversed rib

This pattern forms broad vertical stripes of raised plain stitches with an equal width of reversed stocking stitch in between. It does not have the elasticity of the previous two ribs, because each alternate row is worked as straight purl.

This rib is not suitable as an edging pattern.

Cast on in multiples of six.

Row 1: k3 p3.

Row 2: p.

figure 4.3   Reversed rib

Fisherman's rib

A new variation known as 'knitting below', abbreviated as k1b, is added for this rib stitch. To do this, the right needle is inserted into the bar of the stitch below the next one on the left needle. Knit, then allow both 'stitches' to drop off the needle in the usual way.

Fisherman's rib creates a very warm, lightweight and stretchy fabric, much beloved by action-loving outdoorsy types who need maximum freedom of movement while keeping the elements at bay.

Cast on an even number of stitches.

Row 1: k.

Row 2: k1 k1b to last 2 stitches k2.

Repeat Row 2 as required.

figure 4.4   Fisherman's rib

Wide rib

For this rib, an uneven number of stitches is worked in each set, giving a panelled effect of narrow lines running through the work.

Cast on in multiples of seven.

Row 1: k5 p2. Repeat to the end of the row.

Row 2: k2 p5. Repeat to the end of the row.

(Purl stitches knitted in the previous row and knit stitches previously purled.)

Twisted rib

This is a dense and attractive variation on the simple rib pattern. It has plenty of stretch and gives a slight herringbone effect.

To make a twisted stitch the right needle is inserted into the back instead of the front of the next stitch on the left needle.

Row 1: k1 p1 working into the back of the stitch.

Row 2: p1 k1 working into the back of the stitch.

Moss stitches

Knitters very often declare moss stitch to be their absolute favourite. It is neat and unpretentious, doesn't curl at the edges and has a firm pebbled texture.

It is an ideal stitch for borders on blankets, edgings where buttons are used and for collars. There are plenty of variations but, at its most basic, it is worked on an odd number of stitches as k1 p1 on every row. The knit and purl stitches alternate rather than running in rows as they do with a single rib.

Ordinary moss stitch

The classic much-beloved neat stitch.

Cast on an odd number of stitches.

Row 1: *k1 p1* to last stitch k1.

Repeat this row.

figure 4.5   Wide rib

figure 4.6   Twisted rib

figure 4.7   Ordinary moss

Double moss stitch

This variation is worked over four rows to produce a small diamond pattern.

Cast on an odd number of stitches.

Row 1: k1 *p1 k1* to the end.

Row 2: p1 *k1 p1* to the end.

Row 3: p1 *k1 p1* to the end.

Row 4: k1 *p1 k1* to the end.

Repeat these four rows.

Grille stitch

This version of moss stitch appears complex but it is actually very easy to knit. It has a strong raised squared pattern running over a moss stitch background.

The pattern is worked over four rows and a stitch counter is recommended.

Cast on an odd number of stitches.

Row 1: k to the end.

Row 2: k to the end.

Row 3: *k1 p1* to last stitch k1.

Row 4: k1 p1 to the end.

Four textured patterns
Trinity or blackberry stitch

This pattern has two names. The trinity refers to the method of knitting three stitches into one and then one stitch into three. The second name is more picturesque as the small bobbles resemble a mass of blackberries.

The stitch is one of the traditional Aran patterns worked in panels alongside cables and reverse stocking stitch.

Cast on stitches in multiples of four.

The pattern appears complicated but take it one stage at a time and you will discover that it is actually quite simple.

The k1 p1 k1 into the same stitch means that you do not slip the stitch off the left needle when you knit it, but bring the yarn forward and purl into the same stitch, then take the yarn back and knit into it again. Then allow it to drop off the needle in the normal way.

figure 4.7   Double moss

figure 4.8   Grille

figure 4.9   Trinity or blackberry

Row 1: p to end (RS).

Row 2: k1 *p3tog (k1 p1 k1) all into the same stitch*. Repeat to end.

Row 3: p to end.

Row 4: *p3tog (k1 p1 k1) all into the same stitch*. Repeat to end.

Basketweave stitch

This is a very simple way to add texture to a piece of knitting. It is worked in blocks of four or more stitches but there are no hard and fast rules.

Cast on in multiples of the block size.

These are four stitches wide.

Rows 1–4: k4 p4. Repeat to the end.

Rows 5–8: p4 k4. Repeat to the end.

Betty Martin stitch

Betty Martin was a Guernsey knitter who gave her name to this simple but effective pattern. It has a good texture and is fun to knit. This pattern would have been used in panels on fishermen's sweaters known as 'ganseys'.

Cast on an even number of stitches.

Row 1: k.

Row 2: p.

Row 3: k2 p2.

Row 4: p2 k2.

Lace rib

This is a lovely stitch for a baby blanket or a throw. It has the appearance of expert knitting but all the hard work of the pattern in done in a single row alternated by a straight purl row that gives you time relax and speed up.

Once you have completed several pattern rows your fingers seem to pick up the sequence and it becomes a lot easier.

Cast on in multiples of 10.

Row 1: k1 *yrn k3 sl1 k2tog psso k2 yrn k1*. Repeat to the end.

Row 2: p.

Repeat these two rows to make this lovely pattern.

Abbreviations reminder

k2tog   knit two together to decrease

psso   pass slipped stitch over

sl1   slip one stitch

yrn   yarn round needle

figure 4.10   Basketweave

figure 4.11   Betty Martin

figure 4.12   Lace rib

Cable stitch

Cables are part of the long tradition of knitting fishermen's sweaters using patterns that echo the shapes of ropes and cables on the boats. They are usually knitted in stocking stitch alongside reverse stocking stitch or another textured background stitch that gives them prominence. The twisting patterns appear to demand experience and skill levels beyond the novice knitter, but that is a part of their appeal. It is what makes knitting your first cable such a memorable achievement. Work practice squares of these simple cable patterns in order to understand the method and gain confidence to choose to knit a pattern that features cables:

- Cables are created within a row by placing a set number of stitches onto a short double-pointed cable needle.
- This needle is held at the back or front of the row being worked.

- The same set number of stitches are then knitted from the left needle.
- The stitches on the cable needle are knitted next.
- This creates the twist at the start of the cable by moving stitches from one position in the row to another.

The length of the cable is decided by the number of rows knitted in stocking stitch between the twists.

When the stitches on the cable needle are kept at the **front** of the work the cable will twist the stitches **from right to left**. See Figure 4.13.

When the stitches on the cable needle are kept at the **back** of the work the cable will twist **from left to right**. See Figure 4.14.

Cables are often worked in oppositional pairs.

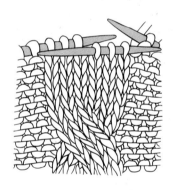

figure 4.13 Cable needle at front

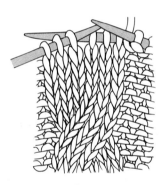

figure 4.14 Cable needle at back

Small cable stitch

Cast on in multiples of five plus three.

Row 1: *p3 k2* to last three stitches p3.

Rows 2–4: stocking stitch

Row 5: *p3 slip 1 onto cable needle and leave at the back of the work k1 then k1 from the cable needle* to last three stitches p3.

Repeat rows 2–5 as required.

Single cable stitch

Cast on in multiples of seven plus three.

Rows 1 and 3: *p3 k4* to last three stitches p3.

Rows 2, 4 and 6: *k3 p4* to last three stitches k3.

Row 5: *p3 slip 2 onto cable needle and leave at the back of the work k2 then k2 from the cable needle* to last three stitches p3.

Repeat as required.

Twisted or coiled rope stitch

This is a bold spiral with a twist to the right.

Cast on in multiples of nine plus three.

Rows 1 and 3: *p3 k6* p3.

Rows 2, 4 and 6: *k3 p6* k3.

Row 5: *p3 slip 3 onto cable needle and leave at the back of the work k3 then k3 stitches from the cable needle* p3.

Repeat as required.

figure 4.15   Small cable

figure 4.16   Single cable

figure 4.17   Twisted cable

Openwork stitches

There was a time when all the babies in the land were dressed in similar lacy knitted outfits lovingly made by their grandmothers. Fashions change and lacy patterns were dropped in favour of plainer more linear styles. Now that retro and vintage have allowed the past back into our lives, an old-fashioned baby shawl or a lacy cashmere cardigan will be given the respect it deserves.

The stitches are more challenging because rows have to be counted, but not all lacework demands the same amount of concentration. The patterns described here are all easy to master and will add another dimension to your knitting. It is a fact that once you have been bitten by the knitting bug, your curiosity will eventually lead you to these more complex knitting patterns. If you avoid pastel colours, the patterns will have a different, more contemporary character.

Lace patterns are made with passed over slipped stitches and yarn over increases followed by decreases to make secure holes. Look at the Abbreviations reminder to recap the terms used to describe these manoeuvres.

Turkish fagotting

This is a deceptively fancy openwork stitch that is easily learned. It is worked as a single repeated pattern row on an even number of stitches.

Row 1: k1 *yfwd k2tog* to last stitch k1.

Repeat as required.

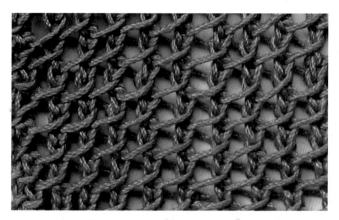

figure 4.18   Turkish fagotting

Abbreviations reminder

k2tog	knit two together to decrease
psso	pass slipped stitch over
sl1	slip one stitch
yfwd	yarn forward between needles
yon	yarn over needle

Cellular stitch

This is a plain open mesh stitch useful for babies' cotton blankets, string bags or beachwear. It features a single repeated pattern row that can be worked on any number of stitches. For best effect, knit this stitch on medium to large needles.

It has a tendency to stretch diagonally and will benefit from being blocked. If used for a baby blanket, a satin ribbon border will help keep the corners square. (See Chapter 3 for an explanation of blocking.)

figure 4.19   Cellular

Single eyelet pattern

This is a pretty stitch best worked in fine yarn and particularly suited to baby clothes in multiples of eight.

Row 1: k.

Row 2 and every alternate row: p.

Row 3: k6 *yon k2tog k6*.

Row 5: k.

Row 7: k2 *yon k2tog k6* to last four stitches k4.

figure 4.20   Single eyelet pattern

Mesh stitch

This is a wide mesh worked as a single repeated pattern row, on an even number of stitches.

Row 1: *yrn sl1 k1 psso*.

Repeat as required.

figure 4.21   Mesh

Motifs and letters

Coloured patterned knitting is usually called Fairisle, although, strictly speaking, the name refers to a particular style of complex and symmetrical patterned knitting.

In Fairisle, no more than two colours are used per row but many more can be used on one garment. True Fairisle is designed to be worked on a circular needle or a set of double-pointed knitting needles. Every row is worked on the right side so colour changes can take place on both odd and even rows.

Working from a chart

A chart is used to make a picture of the pattern or motif to be knitted. This is the easiest way to explain colour changes and to count stitches. Knitting charts are direct descendants of tapestry or Berlin workcharts where each square represented a stitch embroidered on a framed canvas.

When knitting, each square of the grid represents a stitch. The pattern is marked out in colours or alphabetically labelled with a key to relate the colours to the letters.

Charts are read from the bottom upwards reading from right to left on the first and all odd-numbered rows and from left to right on all even-numbered rows.

When knitting in rounds the front of the work is always facing you so the chart is always read from right to left.

You may also come across pattern charts where symbols are used instead of a written pattern with abbreviations. The chart is read in the same way starting at the bottom right corner with every square representing a stitch. A key will explain the symbols.

Designing your own chart

Once you have experimented and have become familiar with chart reading you may want to have a go at designing something of your own. You will need a sheet of tracing paper, a rule, pencil and your pattern motif, letter or numeral to be translated into knitting.

You will also need to relate the design to your knitting. Knit a tension square using the same yarn and needle size to be used for the design. Count the knitted stitches and relate them to the squares on the chart to get a clear idea of the size of your design.

To make a design bolder each element can be worked over a increased number of stitches. Instead of using a single stitch, use two or three to make a broader, more obvious statement.

Draw the grid to match your tension square. If it has 24 stitches over 30 rows to make a 10cm square, then you draw a grid with 24 squares across and 30 squares down on the tracing paper.

Place your motif under the grid and trace its outline.

Fill in all the squares to be knitted either using colours or a symbol to represent the different shades. If only one colour is used mark the chart with an X.

If the design is to be centred, design on an odd number of stitches with the centre square taken as the midpoint.

How to strand the yarn in knit and purl rows

This is the best method to use when knitting the narrow stripes or small colour repeats of Fairisle patterns that use only two colours in any one row. This method should not be used with colour repeats of more than four stitches as it creates loops on the wrong side that could cause pulls and snags.

Knit row

Have both yarns at the back of the work. Knit the stitches required with Yarn A then leave it and pick up and knit with Yarn B. Then pick up Yarn A again. Strand the yarns loosely across the back of the work.

Purl row

Have both yarns at the front of the work and purl the number of stitches for Yarn A then leave it and pick up and purl the number of stitches for Yarn B. Both yarns are stranded loosely across the front of the work – the side facing you.

How to weave the yarn in knit and purl rows

This method is best used when you are working over a larger number of stitches per colour. Instead of stranding the wool straight across behind the row, it is caught by the working yarn after three or four stitches at the back of the work and carried along with it to be taken up in the right place for the next colour change. It is easier to work with two hands. The knitting is done with yarn held in the right hand as usual and the weaving is done with yarn from the left hand.

Knit row

Insert the right needle into the stitch on the left as usual.

Place Yarn B over Yarn A before you knit the stitch. This way it is caught and woven into at the back of the work without actually being knitted. Do not pull the woven yarn too tight or it will show through the front of the work.

Purl row

Insert the right needle into the stitch on the left as usual but before you purl the stitch take Yarn B over Yarn A. Purl the stitch as usual with Yarn A. Yarn B will have been caught and woven neatly along the row without being purled.

Weave the yarn loosely.

Using bobbins

When working on a multicoloured design with patches of colour, it is more practical and easier to use small lengths of yarn wound onto bobbins kept at the back of the work, as opposed to using separate balls, which inevitably become intertwined.

Plastic butterfly-shaped bobbins are specifically made for this purpose and can be bought from any wool supplier or you could cut them out of cardboard.

Keep the bobbin wound right up to the back of the work when it is not in use.

Samples
Chequerboard

figure 4.22   Chequerboard

Black = A.

White = B.

The yarn is stranded loosely across the back of the work, worked over multiples of four stitches.

Cast on using one of the colours.

Rows 1 and 3: k4 A k4 B. Repeat to end of row.

Rows 2 and 4: p4 A p4 B. Repeat to end of row.

Rows 5 and 7: k4 B k4 A. Repeat to end of row.

Rows 6 and 8: p4 B p4 A. Repeat to end of row.

Repeat these eight rows.

The heart motif

Red = A.

White = B.

Worked on an uneven number of stitches.

Cast on in A.

Work as shown on the chart beginning the motif by knitting one stitch in B in the middle of the row. Leave the B yarn at the back.

On the following purl row, pick up the B yarn and purl one stitch before and one stitch after the existing colour B stitch.

Carry B over the A yarn once and then continue the purl row in A.

This 'twist' carries the thread over so that it is in position for the following row and it also helps to keep a smooth line along the edge of the colour change.

Refer to the chart and relate your knitted stitches to the squares.

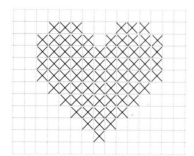

figure 4.23 Heart motif

figure 4.24 Heart motif chart

When the motif is complete snip off the A yarn, allowing enough thread for neat sewing in and complete another four rows of stocking stitch in B.

Knitting a letter

This letter R is worked over five stitches.

Cast on an odd number of stitches.

Green = A.

Pink = B.

Refer to the chart to knit this simple letter.

Weave B over A at the back of the work on the second stitch inside the letter.

figure 4.25 Knitting a letter

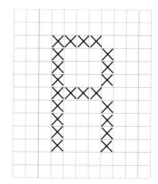

figure 4.26 Letter R chart

The alphabet

The chart below provides a basic A to Z for knitting initials.

Try experimenting on graphpaper to design your own version.

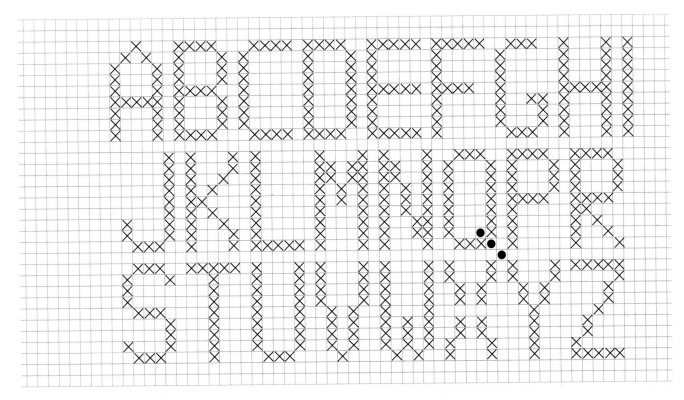

figure 4.27 Alphabet chart

05 the projects

In this chapter you will learn:

- how to knit a garter stitch scarf
- how to knit a striped cotton shoulder bag
- how to knit a chunky cushion cover
- how to knit a ski hat with a pompom
- how to knit a baby's blanket
- how to knit a tasselled hat for a new baby
- how to knit a child's button beanie
- how to knit a jeans-style hat
- how to knit three baby toys
- how to knit a cosy hot water bottle cover
- how to knit a child's Cornish-style sweater
- how to knit a dishcloth
- how to knit a beachbag or large shopper
- how to knit a makeup purse
- how to knit a siesta pillow.

05 the projects

Garter stitch scarf

As soon as you have learned to hold the wool and the needles comfortably and can do the basic knit stitch you are ready to knit a scarf. Plain knit garter stitch is ideal for scarves because it knits up flat and has plenty of stretch.

A simple hand-knitted scarf is comforting in a way that a bought one could never be and if you make a nice long one you will be practising and improving your knitting rhythm and making something at the same time. The more you knit in each knitting session the better your scarf will look because the tension relaxes and becomes more even with repetition and this will create a nice even texture.

The scarf shown here is 140cm long by 15cm wide. Reduce the number of stitches to make a narrower version, knit more rows to make it longer.

A scarf knitted with chunky wool on size 6–7mm needles is a quick, easy and encouraging first project. The fringing is entirely optional, some like it and some don't.

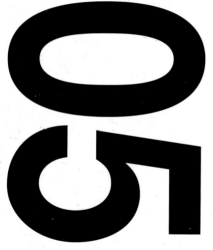

Materials

One 100g ball of chunky yarn

5–6m chunky yarn to match or contrast

Equipment

Pair 7mm needles

Large crochet hook for the fringe

Tension

12 stitches over 12 rows to make a 10cm square.

Pattern

Cast on 18 stitches.

K all rows.

Keep tension moderately loose so that the stitches stay on the needle but can slide along it easily.

Cast off loosely.

Adding a fringe

Cut multiple strands of yarn into twice the depth you want for the fringe. These are 40cm in length to create a 20cm fringe.

Divide them into groups of three strands and fold these in half.

Use the crochet hook to draw the folded ends through spaces between stitches in the row above the cast-off edge and make a loop.

Use the crochet hook to draw the long strands through this loop. Pull them up firmly to make a knot at the top.

Repeat this at regular intervals along the same side of the work.

Trim with sharp scissors to level the fringe.

figure 5.1   Keep a friend warm in winter
(opposite)

Striped cotton shoulder bag

Choose nice chunky cotton yarn and two or more of your favourite colours to knit yourself a funky new bag. The bag is worked in a single piece starting at the bottom on long needles and knitting it as deep as you like, then casting off on both sides to work on eight remaining stitches in the middle, which form the strap.

The bag is then folded in half and sewn along the base and side seam. The end of the strap is stitched in place across the top of the side seam.

Materials

One ball each of chunky cotton yarn in orange and lime. Or use a double strand of any DK hand-knitting cotton

Equipment

Pair 5mm needles

Tapestry needle

Tension

15 stitches over 15 rows to make a 10cm square.

Pattern

Cast on 50 stitches using the green yarn.

Work in knit stitch throughout, keeping the tension as even as you can.

K six rows.

*Leave the green yarn at the edge and k the next two rows with the orange yarn. Now leave this yarn at the edge.

Pick up the green yarn and k the next two rows in green and leave it again.

Pick up the orange yarn and k the next two rows then break the yarn.*

Pick up the green and continue knitting with it for the next 10 rows.

Now repeat from * – *.

K another 10 rows using the green yarn.

Repeat from * – *.

K a further two rows of green then cast off 22 stitches, k the following eight stitches and cast off the remaining 22 stitches.

Rejoin the work using the green yarn and k a further 84 rows on the eight stitches to make the shoulder strap. The strap can be made firmer if you knit into the back of the loop to make a twisted knit stitch, rather than knitting into the front in the usual way.

Making up

Block and press the bag.

Thread a length of green cotton onto a wide-eyed needle and sew up the bag beginning at the top and working down the side seam and across the base. Secure the yarn and weave it into the work. Stitch the strap securely to the top of the bag so that it sits across the side seam. Weave the remaining thread into the knitting on the inside of the bag.

Adding a lining

The bag will be even more useful if you make a cotton lining.

Add 4cm both ways to the actual measurements of the bag.

Cut out two pieces of fabric according to those measurements.

Stitch them together leaving the top end open.

Keep the raw edges on the outside and slip the lining inside the bag.

The top edge seam can be folded in towards the knitting and slipstitched to the inside top edge of the bag.

figure 5.2 Garter stitch has a thick rippled texture
(opposite)

Chunky knit cushion cover

Big needles and super chunky wool mean that one of these stylish cushion covers can be made in an evening. The pure wool used here creates an invitingly soft and luxurious place to rest your head. Simple stocking stitch gives a smooth finish and the garter stitch flap adds a textural contrast. Make sure the buttons are large enough to suit the cushion proportions.

Materials
Three 100g balls of super chunky wool in a rust colour
3 large buttons

Equipment
Pair 12mm needles
Tapestry needle

Tension
8 stitches over 10 rows to make a 10cm square.

Pattern
Cast on 34 stitches.

Row 1: k.

Row 2: p.

Repeat till the work measures 68cm (about 70 rows).

Change to garter stitch and k four rows.

Buttonhole row
k4 sl1 k3tog psso k6 sl1 k3tog psso k6 sl1 k3tog psso k4.

K another four rows and cast off loosely.

Making up
Block and press very lightly.

Turn the cover inside out and sew up the side seams using backstitch.

Mark the positions for the buttons and use a finer yarn to stitch them in place.

Fill the cover with a cushion pad and ... relax.

figure 5.3 Large vintage buttons give a stylish finish *(opposite)*

Ski hat with a pompom

There is something undeniably cute about a knitted hat with a pompom – especially when the pompom is as large and sassy as this one. The hat is knitted on four needles, which can seem a bit unwieldy at the beginning but using chunky wool ensures that it grows quickly. Four-needle knitting is easier once you have knitted a few rows so don't give up, persevere and you will soon get into the rhythm of it.

This project is all in rib stitch.

Materials

One ball chunky bright pink wool

One ball chunky white wool

Equipment

Set of four double-pointed 6mm needles

Tapestry needle

Two 12cm circles of card (cereal boxes are ideal)

Pair of sharp scissors

Abbreviations reminder

k2 p2   knit two purl two rib

k2tog   knit two together

sl1   slip one stitch

Tension

12 stitches over 18 rows to make a 10cm square.

Pattern

Cast 60 stitches onto one of the needles.

Note: I always cast on using the thumb method for hats as it gives a neat edge that is firm and stretchy.

Now divide these stitches equally over three of the needles, slipping 30 stitches onto each one.

k2 p2 rib on the next and all following rows until shaping is required.

Form the needles into a triangle and use the spare fourth needle to knit the first stitch that will join the circle.

Note: Keep the tension quite tight for the first couple of k stitches to avoid any looping or sagging at the join. At this point you will wish you have two pairs of hands but it will soon get easier.

Continue with this ribbing stitch until the knitting measures at least 18 cm in length.

Shaping

1st round: k2tog p2, repeat (45 stitches remain).

2nd round: p2tog k1, repeat (30 stitches remain).

3rd round: k2tog, repeat (15 stitches).

4th round: k2tog (7 stitches).

Thread the yarn onto the needle and pull the thread through the remaining seven stitches to draw the circle together and sew the yarn end into the top.

Weave any loose ends into the inside of the hat and snip off the loose ends.

Making the pompom

Cut out two circles of card measuring 12cm across (diameter).

Cut a 3cm circle out of the middle of each one to make two rings.

Cut several 2m lengths of pink and white yarn and use the needle to thread the yarn double.

Hold the two rings together as you wind the yarn evenly around them until the hole in the middle fills up.

Insert the point of the scissors at the edge between the two pieces of card and cut through the yarn all around the outside edge.

Pull the two circles just slightly apart so that you can tie a piece of yarn tightly between them, keeping these ends long enough to be used for stitching the pompom to the hat.

Cut the card away and remove it.

Fluff up the pompom and trim it to make a nice round shape, then thread the yarn and sew the pompom firmly to the top of the hat.

figure 5.4 A rasberry and vanilla pompom hat *(opposite)*

Baby's blanket

Keep a newborn baby snug and warm by knitting this simple cover that can be used on a pram, crib or tucked around a buggy. The pattern has a moss stitch border and a patchwork of stocking stitch and reverse stocking stitch, all knitted as one piece. A handmade blanket makes a lovely gift and can be made in advance as you don't have to consider the baby's size or to colour code it for a boy or a girl. This one was knitted in a cream DK wool on a size 5 circular needle used in the conventional way. The circular needles work well for heavier items like blankets because the weight of the knitting can rest in your lap instead of being carried on the needles.

If you would prefer to knit in a finer baby yarn, it is very important to work a tension sample and adjust the needle size for the weight of the wool.

This border is in moss stitch.

Materials
Four 50g balls of cream double knitting wool

Equipment
Size 4–5 circular needle
Or a pair of size 4–5 long needles

Abbreviations reminder

k   knit

m   moss stitch

p   purl

Tension
9 stitches and 11 rows to make a 5cm square.

Pattern
Cast on 80 stitches.

Work 10 rows in k1 p1 moss stitch.

For the main part of the pattern, moss stitch x 10 at beginning and end of every row.

Next row: *m10 k15 p15 k15 p15 m10.

Next row: m10 p15 k15 p15 k15 m10*.

Repeat these two rows nine times.

Next row: *m10 p15 k15 p15 k15 m10.

Next row: m10 k15 p15 k15 p15 m10*.

Repeat these two rows nine times.

Repeat these two pattern blocks three more times so that the blanket is four panels wide and eight panels long.

Work 10 rows in k1 p1 moss stitch and cast off loosely.

Making up
Weave the yarn ends into the rows and trim the ends.

Block and press the blanket using a warm iron and a damp cloth.

figure 5.5   Moss stitch gives the blanket a nice flat edge
(opposite)

Tasselled hat for a new baby

Many of us first feel the urge to knit when we or our friends have babies. It is a fact that people who have never given knitting a thought before suddenly feel the urge to pick up a pair of needles and knit hats and booties. It must be something vaguely biological that precedes the urge to push!

Few can resist the lure of knitting in miniature as everything takes less time, less yarn and earns the most applause. Babies also look incredibly cute in beanie hats.

The instructions here are for a hat knitted on two needles with a back seam and the style makes a feature of the natural hem roll-over that happens with stocking stitch.

Materials

One 50g ball fine baby yarn

Equipment

Pair 3.75 mm needles

Sewing-up needle

Small piece of card for the tassel

Size

To fit a newborn baby 0–3 months.

Tension

24 stitches over 32 rows to make a 10cm square.

Pattern

Cast on 60 stitches.

Row 1: k.

Row 2: p.

Repeat the first two rows (stocking stitch) until the work measures 15cm, ending with a p row.

Shaping

Row 1: k8 k2tog. Repeat to end of row.

Row 2: p.

Row 3: k.

Row 4: k7 k2tog. Repeat to end of row.

Row 5: p.

Row 6: k.

Row 7: p.

Row 8: k6 k2tog. Repeat to end of row.

Row 9: p.

Row 10: k.

Row 11: p.

Row 12: k5 k2tog. Repeat to end of row.

Row 13: p.

Row 14: k.

Row 15: p.

Row 16: k4 k2tog. Repeat to end of row.

Row 17: p.

Row 18: k2tog. Repeat to end of row.

Row 19: p.

Row 20: k2tog. Repeat to end of row.

Now break off the yarn, thread the needle and draw it though the remaining stitches, overstitching the end to secure it.

Making up

Line up the two edges to be joined with the hat inside out and pin them together. Thread the yarn ends onto the sewing needle and use them to sew up the hat to within 5cm of the bottom edge. Turn the hat the right way around and sew up the last 5cm to the bottom edge. This gives the roll-over edge at the bottom a neat finish.

The tassel

Cut a piece of card 10cm × 5cm.

Wind the yarn around the long length of the card 20 times (less for a thinner and more for a thicker tassel). Thread the needle and draw it under the yarn at the top of the card and tie a secure knot. Remove the card, wind the threaded yarn around the top of the tassel several times to make a small ball at the top then stitch through from middle to top once or twice to secure it. Now cut the loops at the bottom and trim to a neat shape. Sew this to the top of the hat.

figure 5.6 Practise your tassel-making skills
(opposite)

Child's button beanie

This child's beanie is knitted in the round on four needles. Every round is worked as knit or plain on the right side of the work but you get the effect of stocking stitch in which every alternate row is purl.

The hat rolls up around the edge and is finished off with a button on the top.

Materials

Two 50g balls double knitting wool or cotton/wool mix
One button for the top of the hat

Equipment

Set of four double-pointed 4mm knitting needles

Size

To fit a child 5–7 years. Make bigger size adjustments by increments of 10 stitches (5cm) and add rows to the main body of the hat to adjust its depth.

Tension

20 stitches × 32 rows to make a 10cm square.

Pattern

Cast on 90 stitches. The thumb method will give a neat elastic edge.

Divide these evenly onto three needles so that each has 30 stitches.

Hold the needles in a triangle and use the fourth needle to begin knitting.

Pull the wool quite firmly when making the first stitch to avoid any loop forming at the join. The beginning of the round can be marked with a coloured marker ring or by noting the position of the cast-on tail end.

K in rounds until the knitting measures 14cm.

Shaping

The hat is shaped by using the k2tog decrease at regular intervals.

Round 1: k9 k2tog. Repeat to end of row.

Round 2: k.

Round 3: k8 k2tog. Repeat to end of row.

Round 4: k.

Round 5: k7 k2 tog. Repeat to end of row.

Round 6: k.

Round 7: k6 k2tog. Repeat to end of row.

Round 8: k.

Round 9: k5 k2tog. Repeat to end of row.

Round 10: k.

Round 11: k2tog. Repeat to end of row.

Round 12: k.

Round 13: k2 tog. Repeat to end of row.

Making up

Break the yarn off and thread it onto a darning needle.

Thread this through the remaining stitches and pull tight to close the opening.

Stitch the ends into the wrong side of the work.

Sew a button onto the top of the hat.

figure 5.7 Practise knitting in the round
(opposite)

Jeans-style hat

The denim yarn used for this hat is designed to fade the way jeans do and the orange cotton detail of the hat mimics the seam stitching of blue jeans. The pattern is knitted on two needles with a back seam but four double-pointed needles or a circular needle could be substituted if you prefer not to do any sewing up.

This hat is a beanie style with a rolled edge that doesn't cover the ears.

For those whose ears are prone to feel the cold, work the straight section at least 10cm longer before beginning to decrease to shape the crown.

Materials
One 100g ball of chunky denim-look wool or cotton
Small ball of orange chunky cotton yarn

Equipment
Pair 6mm needles
Sewing-up needle

Abbreviations reminder

k   knit

k2tog   knit two together

p   purl

st st   stocking stitch

Tension

14 stitches and 18 rows to make a 10cm square.

Pattern

Use the thumb method to cast on 72 stitches.

Try to master the thumb method as it makes a firm but stretchy edging ideal for hats.

Row 1: k.

Row 2: p.

Repeat these rows working in st st until the work measures 14cm from the start, ending on a knit row. Break the yarn.

*Work the p row using the orange cotton then break the yarn.

Rejoin the denim yarn*.

Work a further five rows st st ending with a k row.

Break the yarn.

Repeat * – *.

K five rows of st st ending with a p row.

Shaping

Row 1: k1 *k12 k2tog (×5)* k1 (67 stitches remain).

Row 2: p.

Row 3: k1 *k11 k2tog (×5)* k1 (62 stitches remain).

Row 4: p.

Row 5: k1 *k10 k2tog (×5)* k1 (57 stitches remain).

Row 6: p.

Row 7: k1 *k9 k2tog (×5)* k1 (52 stitches remain).

Row 8: p.

Row 9: k1 *k8 k2tog (×5)* k1 (47 stitches remain).

Row 10: p.

Row 11: k1 *k7 k2tog (×5)* k1 (42 stitches remain).

Row 12: p.

Row 13: k1 *k2tog (× 20)* k1   (22 stitches remain).

Row 14: p.

Row 15: k2tog (×11).

Break the yarn and thread the wool through the remaining stitches and pull them firmly together.

Stitch the end to secure it on the wrong side of the crown.

Making up

Use a large sewing-up needle to weave all the yarn ends into the inside of the hat and sew up the back seam neatly, stitching on the right side for the last 3cm or 4cm where the rim rolls over.

figure 5.8   Modern wools have helped to kick-start the knitting revival
(opposite)

Baby toys

Small babies will love these soft textures and bright shapes. If you are making all three toys buy six different colours of yarn; otherwise use up oddments of washable baby-friendly yarn. If you would like to add noise to the toys put a few dry beans inside a plastic film canister and bury it in the middle of the filling.

The ball

This ball has a diameter of 14cm.

Materials

Six different coloured balls of cotton DK yarn
Washable toy filling

Equipment

Pair size 3.75mm needles
Pair of scissors
Sewing-up needle

figure 5.9 Simple shapes for baby's hands

Pattern

Cast on two stitches.

Row 1: p.

Row 2: cast on 1 k2 cast on 1 (4 stitches).

Row 3: p.

Row 4: cast on 1 k4 cast on 1 (6 stitches).

Row 5: p.

Row 6: cast on 1 k6 cast on 1 (8 stitches).

Row 7: p.

Row 8: cast on 1 k8 cast on 1 (10 stitches).

Row 9: p.

Row 10: cast on 1 k10 cast on 1 (12 stitches).

Work eight rows in st st (k one row p one row).

Continue in stocking stitch but k2tog at the beginning and end of every knit row until only one stitch remains.

Break yarn, leaving it long enough for sewing up the side, thread it through the loop and pull it up tight.

Change colour and knit five more shapes the same as this.

Making up

Use the yarn ends to sew sections of the ball together on the wrong side. When only one seam remains sew halfway, turn the ball right side out and stuff the ball with the filling. Don't be mean with it, as the fuller it is the better the shape will be.

Sew up the last section of seam neatly from the outside and poke the needle through the ball to hide the yarn end safely inside.

figure 5.10 Bright colours for a toy basket *(opposite)*

The cube

This cube has been knitted in plain colours but even more fun can be had by knitting coloured stripes; creating different pattern textures or knitting motifs or letters. This is quite a large cube and the size can easily be adjusted by using fewer stitches to make the squares.

Materials
Six different coloured cotton DK yarn
Washable toy filling

Equipment
Pair 3.75mm needles
Sewing-up needle

Pattern

The cube's sides measure 12cm × 12cm.

Cast on 24 stitches.

Row 1: k.

Row 2: p.

Repeat these two rows 16–18 more times, depending on your tension.

When the shape is square cast off.

Break the yarn, leaving it long enough for sewing up the side, thread it through the loop and pull it up tight.

Repeat five more times using a different colour for each one.

Making up

Use the yarn ends and matching yarns to sew the sides of the cube together, on the wrong side, leaving half of one side open.

Turn the cube right side out and stuff it with the filling.

Finally, sew up the seam neatly on the outside and poke the needle through to hide the yarn end inside the cube.

The pyramid

One square and four triangles are knitted to make a sturdy pyramid. The sides can either be worked on stitches picked up from the edges of the square base or they can be knitted as individual triangles to be sewn to the base afterwards. The individual method is described here.

Materials
Five different coloured cotton DK yarns
Washable toy filling

Equipment
Pair 3.75mm needles
Sewing-up needle

Abbreviations reminder

k   knit

k2tog knit two together

p   purl

Pattern

For the base: cast on 24 stitches and work a st st square as shown for the cube.

For the sides: cast on 24 stitches.

Row 1: p.

Row 2: k2tog *k*. until last two stitches k2tog.

Repeat these two rows until only one stitch remains.

Break the yarn, leaving it long enough for sewing up the side, thread it through the loop and pull it up tight.

Repeat three more times using different colours.

Making up

Sew all the pieces together from the wrong side leaving half of one seam open. Turn and stuff the shape with filling.

Finally, sew up the rest of the seam neatly and poke the needle through the middle of the shape to hide the yarn end safely inside.

figure 5.11   Practise your making up skills
(opposite)

Cosy hot water bottle cover

There is nothing to beat an old-fashioned hot water bottle for instant comfort and defrosting on a cold winter's night. Show your hot water bottle how much you love it by knitting this soft cabled polo neck sweater to double its huggability. Sentiment aside, a knitted cover will prevent a hot water bottle from scalding and also keep its heat for much longer.

Materials

Two 50g balls of chunky wool or wool/cashmere mix

Equipment

Pair 5.5mm needles
Cable needle
Sewing-up needle

Tension

14 stitches over 22 rows to make a 10cm square.

Pattern

Front

Cast on 42 stitches.

Row 1: k18, slip three stitches onto a cable needle and hold them at the back of the work. K the next three stitches on the left-hand needle in the usual way then k the three stitches from the cable needle.

Row 2: p.

Row 3: k.

Row 4: p.

Repeat rows 1–4 until the work measures 25cm.

Shoulder shaping

Row 1: sl1 k2tog psso k to end of row.

Row 2: s11 p2tog psso p to end of row.

Repeat these two rows. You now have 38 stitches.

Polo neck

Cast off nine stitches then work 20 stitches in k1 p1 rib then cast off the nine stitches that remain on the needle.

Rejoin the wool and work 12cm of k1 p1 rib then cast off.

Making up

Sew up all the seams apart from the polo-neck opening.

Fold an empty hot water bottle in half and insert it through the stretchy neck opening.

Carefully fill with hot water and snuggle up.

figure 5.12   The ribbed neck fits snugly but will stretch to insert the hot water bottle *(opposite)*

Child's Cornish-style sweater

'Gansey' patterns initially appear more complex than they are when broken down into their component parts. This one is no exception. This fisherman's-style sweater for a young child has been designed to practise stitches and techniques described in the book.

The panels are stocking stitch, moss, grille, rib and a very simple cable section all framed inside a garter stitch border.

The wide shape will allow a wriggly toddler plenty of room to manoeuvre and the generous neck opening will make it easy to get on and off.

Materials

Seven 50g balls of 4 ply wool/cotton mix

figure 5.13   Practise your cable stitch

Equipment

Three 3.25mm needles

3.25mm circular needle

Two large stitch holders

Medium-sized cable needle

Abbreviation reminder

m1   make one – increase by knitting into both front and back of next stitch

Size

To fit a child aged 2–3 years.

The neck and chest measurements are generous. To make the garment for a 4 year old increase the length of the sleeves and body by increasing the number of rows knitted in the stocking stitch sections of the front, back and the sleeves.

Measurements

Shoulder to hem: 36cm

Sleeves: 25cm

Across chest: 34cm

Across back: 34cm

Around neck: 40cm

Tension

22 stitches and 30 rows to make a 10 cm square.

Pattern

Back and front

Cast on 78 stitches using 3.25mm needles and work 10 rows garter stitch.

Work four rows of k2 p2 rib keeping the first and last six stitches k.

Continue working in st st until the work measures 22cm, keeping the first six and last six stitches k and ending with a p row.

Commence pattern.

Moss stitch panel
Row 1: k6 *k1 p1* to last six stitches k6.

Row 2: k6 *p1 k1* to last six stitches k6.

Repeat these rows twice more (six rows altogether).

Cable panel
Row 1: k6 *p3 k4* to last nine stitches p3 k6.

Row 2: k6 *k3 p4* to last nine stitches k9.

Row 3: as Row 1.

Row 4: as Row 2.

Row 5: k6 *p3 sl2 onto cable needle and leave at the back of work k2 then k2 from the cable needle*. Repeat to last nine stitches p3 k6.

Row 6: as row 2.

Repeat these six rows three times (18 rows altogether).

Stocking stitch the next four rows keeping the first and last six stitches k.

Grille stitch panel
Row 1: k.

Row 2: k.

Row 3: k6 *k1 p1* to last six stitches k.

Row 4: k6 *k1 p1* to last six stitches k.

Repeat these four rows four times.

Do not cast off; keep stitches on the needle.

Sleeves (make two!)
Cast on 40 stitches using 3.25 needles.

K1 row.

Work in k2 p2 rib until work measures 5cm.

Shaping
Continue in st st as follows:

Next row: k2 m1 knit to last two stitches m1 k2.

Work one row.

Increase as before on next and then every fourth row until there are 68 stitches on the needle.

Continue in st st without further shaping until the work measures 21cm from beginning.

Next row: k2 p2 rib to end.

Repeat this row six times.

Cast off in k.

Shoulders and neck
The shoulders are joined by knitting the back and front sections together using a third needle. Line up the two pieces of knitting with the needle points facing the same way and the wrong sides facing each other.

K2tog through first two loops taking one stitch from each needle.

Repeat with next two loops again taking one stitch from each needle.

Cast off first stitch.

Continue in this way until 14 stitches have been cast off from each needle.

Break off the yarn and slip next 50 stitches from front onto a stitch holder.

Slip 50 stitches from the back onto another stitch holder.

Rejoin wool and work the second shoulder as before.

Slip stitches from both holders onto the circular needle (100 stitches altogether).

Knit eight rounds of k2 p2 rib casting off loosely in rib.

Making up
Block and press lightly.

Sew sleeves into the armholes matching the centre of the sleeve with the shoulder seam.

Join side seams and sleeve seams together using a backstitch.

Leave the garter stitch rows at the hem open to form a split.

Dishcloth patterns

You want me to knit a dishcloth? 'Life's too short' I hear you cry! I say, give it a try.

All of us get through mountains of washing-up cloths, sponges and brushes in the course of our lifetime, using them everyday with little or no thought to what they look like or how long they last.

Knitted cotton cloths are different. They do the job really well because they are absorbent; rough cotton is strong and mildly abrasive; they can be put through the washing machine to freshen up and the openwork patterns allow air to circulate through so that they also dry easily. And being made of natural cotton they are less likely to be whiffy.

This is also an ideal way to practise your lacy and openwork knitting patterns.

figure 5.14   Practise your openwork knitting stitches

Dishcloths and washcloths don't have to be very big and you will find that even complex patterns that require intense concentration will not take very long to knit.

Make them for friends and you will be amazed at how much they are appreciated. And the better they look, the happier you will feel when you do those dishes ...

Knitting dishcloths can be a positive life-enhancing experience!

Spread the word.

Turkish openwork cloth

This is also known as Turkish faggoting. The pattern is very simple and is worked over one row that is repeated until the required length is reached.

Bands of garter stitch worked within the cloth help to keep the square shape.

> **Materials**
> One ball of dishcloth cotton
>
> **Equipment**
> Pair of 5mm needles
> Use large sizes to make bigger holes or smaller for a tighter texture

Pattern

Cast on 40 stitches quite loosely.

Row 1: k1 *yfwd k2tog*. Repeat to last stitch k1.

Repeat this row to form the main pattern.

Work five more rows of pattern then six rows of garter stitch or plain knitting.

Work 18 pattern rows then six rows of garter stitch.

Work six rows of pattern and cast off loosely.

Lace rib cloth

This makes a very pretty patterned cloth with a scalloped edge. It would also make a nice facecloth but it would need to be knitted in a softer DK cotton yarn.

Once again, and surprisingly as it appears very complex, the pattern is worked as a single row with a purl row between that gives you a chance to pick up speed and take your eyes off the knitting.

Materials
One ball of dishcloth cotton or soft DK cotton for a facecloth

Equipment
Pair 4–5mm needles (the smaller size gives a tighter texture)

Pattern

The pattern is worked as any number of stitches divisible by 10 plus one extra stitch.

Cast on 41 stitches.

Row 1: k1 *yrn k3 sl1 k2tog psso k2 yrn k1*. Repeat to end.

Row 2: p.

Repeat these two rows until you have knitted a square, then cast off loosely.

Garter stitch pot holder

Protect your hands when lifting something hot in the kitchen by using one of these thick cotton pot holders. The yarn is used double here to add bulk to the knitting.

Materials
One ball of dishcloth cotton

Equipment
Pair 4–5mm needles (the smaller size makes a denser fabric)

Pattern

Unwind half the cotton ball and rewind to give you two smaller balls.

Cast on 30 stitches using both balls to double the yarn thickness.

Knit 24 rows in garter stitch then cast off.

Betty Martin pattern

Betty Martin was a Guernsey knitter who gave her name to this simple but effective pattern. It is not strictly openwork but has a good texture and is fun to knit. This pattern would have been used on fishermen's sweaters but it adapts well to the dishcloth format. The edges are picked up and knitted with stitch increases at the corners.

Materials
Dishcloth cotton

Equipment
Pair 4mm needles
Sewing-up needle for loose ends

Pattern

Cast on an even number of stitches.

Row 1: k.

Row 2: p.

Row 3: k2 p2.

Row 4: p2 k2.

Repeat this sequence until you have a nice square cloth.

Edging

Pick up and knit an equal even number of stitches from one edge.

Row 1: cast on one stitch then k to the end and cast on one extra stitch.

Row 2: k to end.

Repeat these two rows twice more and cast off.

Repeat on the other three sides then stitch up the corners and weave the loose ends into the fabric of the cloth.

Beachbag or large shopper

This large bag is knitted using mesh stitch with cotton tape on big needles. Decide on a shopping or beach trip and knit the bag you need in a couple of days. The openwork style makes this particularly good for carrying damp beach clothes and towels. This number of stitches makes a big 40cm × 40cm bag but the same pattern can be used to make a smaller version – simply cast on fewer stitches and follow the same instructions.

The bag is very easy to line. Simply cut two pieces of fabric to match the bag size and machine stitch side and base seams. Turn a hem over at the top and slipstitch it to the inside top edge of the knitted bag.

Knitted handles do have a tendency to stretch so you may want to line the handle in matching fabric and stitch it to the bag lining.

Materials
Five 50g balls of chunky cotton tape

Equipment
Pair 10mm needles for the bag
Pair 7mm needles for the strap
Very large sewing-up needle

Abbreviations reminder

garter stitch   every row k

moss stitch   row 1: k1 p1; row 2: p1 k1

psso   pass slipped stitch over

sl1   slip one stitch

yrn   yarn round needle

Beginner's guide to mesh stitch

- Hold the needles as if you were about to knit into the first stitch but instead make a stitch on the right needle by wrapping the yarn once around it.

- Now slip the first stitch from the left needle onto the right needle next to the wrapped stitch.

- Knit the following stitch.

- Use the left needle to lift the middle, slipped stitch, over the last knitted stitch and off the needle.

Pattern

Cast on 50 stitches.

Row 1: *yrn sl1 k1 psso*.

Try to complete each row without interruptions but if you do have to stop you can see whether your last stitch is a wrapped or knitted one. Wrapped stitches slant whereas knitted ones sit straight on the needle.

Repeat this pattern row until the work measures 38 cm.

Now k next four rows (plain knitting) then cast off.

Knit another piece in the same way.

Strap
Using the 7mm needles, cast on eight stitches and work six rows of moss stitch.

Row 1: k1 p1.

Row 2: p1 k1.

Change to garter stitch until work measures 55cm.

Now work six rows in moss stitch and cast off.

Making up

Thread a long length of cotton tape onto the needle and sew up three sides of the bag.

Stitch the strap to the sides so that the strap straddles the joined edges.

Optional lining instructions
Lay the bag on a sheet of newspaper and draw the shape, then using this as a template, cut two pieces of fabric to line the bag and a long strip to line the strap. Make a French seam by sewing close to the edge on the right side to join the fabric pieces, then, turning them the other way out, press the seams and sew another seam 1cm from the edge. This tucks away all the raw edges and prevents fraying.

The lining can now be put inside the bag and hem stitched along the top inside edge. The strap lining can either be machined by sewing with the fabric side upwards or simply hem stitched to the knitted strap and the top of the lining fabric.

Makeup purse

Knit a pretty and practical makeup purse in washable cotton in stocking stitch with a decorative heart pattern. The purse is triangular in shape so that it sits flat on a dressing table and it is compact enough to carry around in your handbag.

The hearts are worked from the chart provided where every square represents a stitch. This one has been fitted with a light cotton lining and a zip. The purse can also be left unlined with the zip slipstitched into the knitted edge as we saw earlier.

If you have not knitted a motif like this before, it is a good idea to do a practice square.

The knack of making successful mid-row colour changes is to concentrate on keeping the same yarn tension as you do for the rest of the knitting, otherwise the heart shape will distort. Too loose and the shape will be baggy, too tight and it will appear pinched.

Materials
Knitted in twisted glazed 3ply cotton
Two balls bright pink
One ball cream

Equipment
Pair 3.25mm needles

Tension
24 stitches over 32 rows to make a 10cm square.

Pattern
Base
Cast on 67 stitches.

Row 1: k.

Row 2: p.

Continue work in st st for 12cm and cast off.

Triangular end piece (make two!)
Cast on 28 stitches in bright pink.

Row 1: k.

Row 2: p.

Row 3: k1 k2tog k to last three stitches then k2tog and k1.

Row 4: p.

Repeat 3rd and 4th rows until four stitches remain, then cast off.

figure 5.15   Pretty and practical – and all your own work

Sides (make two!)
Cast on 67 stitches.

Row 1: k.

Row 2: p.

Repeat these two rows (st st) for eight rows.

Begin heart pattern detail: k13 stitches then insert pattern as shown on the chart then k13 stitches to the end of the row.

Follow the pattern as shown on the chart.

Work another eight rows st st and cast off.

Making up

Making the lining
Block and press the individual knitted pieces. Draw a paper pattern of each of the shapes (2 × ends; 1 × base; 2 × sides), add a 2cm seam allowance and cut out a cotton lining. Machine stitch the seams leaving the long top seam open.

Making up the purse
Lay the two long side pieces flat and pin the zip between them. Stitch the zip in place before making up the purse. Now stitch the ends to the sides. Undo the zip and turn the work inside out and stitch the base in place. Turn the work again so that it is right side out.

Fitting the lining
Turn the lining so that the seams are on the outside and place it inside the knitted purse. Turn over a small hem tucking it between the lining and the knitting and slipstitch the lining in place.

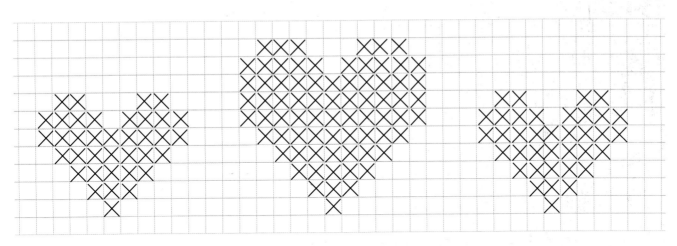

figure 5.16   Makeup bag chart

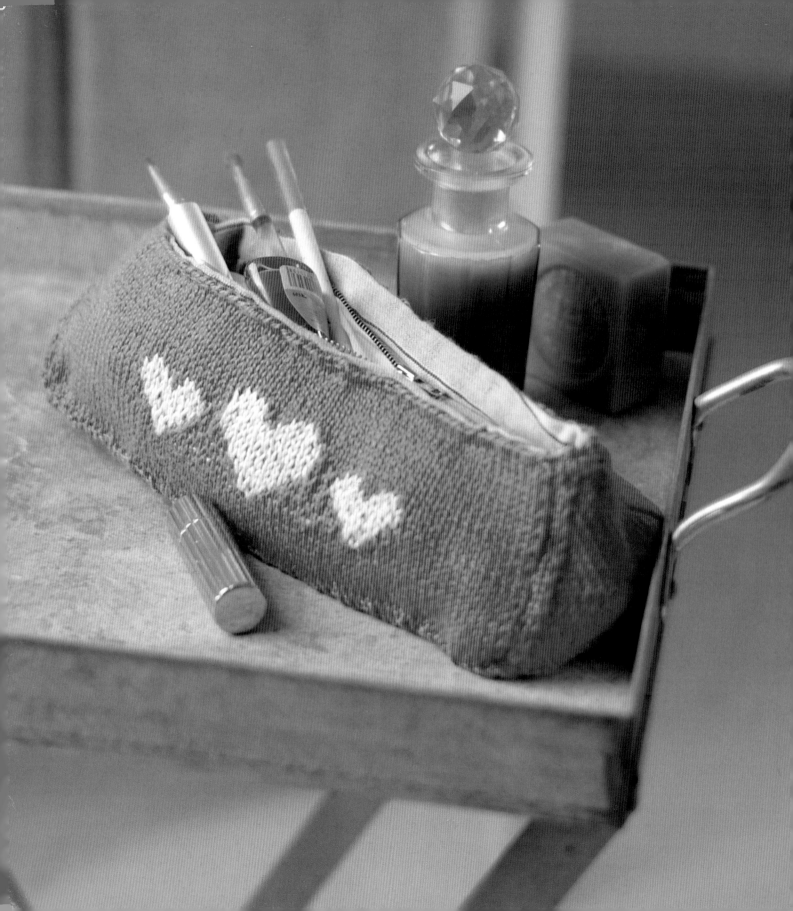

Siesta pillow

Use this whenever you want to take a catnap.

This little cushion would make a perfect gift for a friend who is inclined to take a little siesta after lunch. The pattern is easy to knit and the alphabet is a very simple one suitable for a beginner. The two colours used here create a vibrant contrast (a bit more fiesta than siesta) but the effect can be softened by choosing softer harmonizing colours like pink and lilac.

Equipment
Pair 3.25mm needles
Sewing-up needle

Size
Makes a 30cm × 20cm cushion cover.

Tension
24 stitches over 29 rows to make a 10cm square.

Abbreviations reminder

k   knit

p   purl

Rs   right side facing

st st   stocking stitch

Materials
Two 50g balls of main colour red 4 ply mercerized cotton

One 50g ball of pattern colour blue 4 ply mercerized cotton

30cm × 20cm cushion pad or fabric and polyester/kapok filling

figure 5.18   Somewhere for a friend to rest their head

Pattern

Red colour = A.

Blue colour = B.

Front

Using A, cast on 71 stitches.

Work 4cm in st st, beginning with a k row finishing on a p row.

Row 1: Rs *k1A k1B*. Repeat to end of row.

Row 2: p1B p1A. Repeat to end of row.

Work four rows st st in B.

Row 3: k1A k3B. Repeat to end of row.

Row 4: p1B *p1A p3B*. Repeat to end of row.

Row 4: kA.

Row 5: pA.

Work four rows in st st in B.

Use the chart for the following nine rows to knit 'zzz SIESTA zzz'.

Each square represents one stitch.

Work four rows in st st in B.

Row 15: pA.

Row 16: kA.

Row 17: p3A p1B. Repeat to end of row.

Row 18: k1B *k1A k3B*. Repeat to end of row.

Work four rows in st st in B.

Row 19: p1A p1B. Repeat to end of row.

Row 20: k1B k1A. Repeat to end of row.

Work 4cm in st st in A and cast off.

Back

Cast on 72 stitches and work in st st in A until work measures 20cm.

Measure it against the front and adjust by adding or subtracting a row or two if necessary, then cast off.

Making up

Block and press the two pieces.

Join one short side and two long sides then insert the cushion pad and stitch the last side neatly.

Now ... take a nap. You've earned it after these projects!

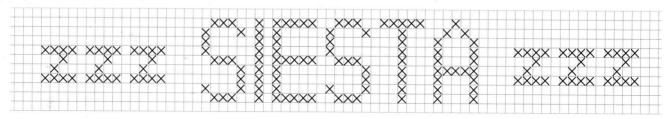

figure 5.17   Siesta pillow chart

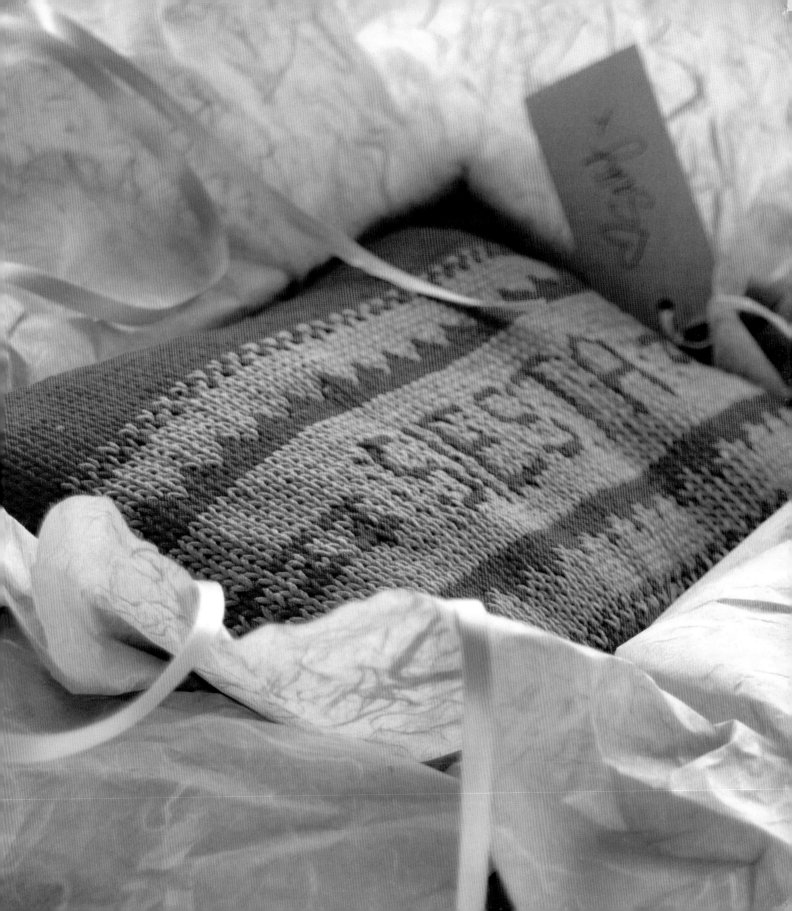

06 now that you can knit ...

In this chapter you will learn:

- about knitting together
- knitting tips and how to progress
- about yarn suppliers.

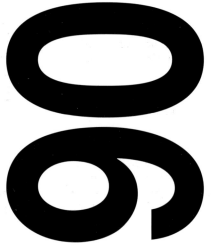

now that you can knit ...

Knitting together
The knitting group

Knitting as a group activity seems a strange concept until you try it, then you understand and realize what has been missing from your life.

Knitting groups are for busy people who do not usually justify taking time for themselves. These multi-taskers are often too caught up with their jobs/partners/homes/gardens/kids/chores to spend a couple of relaxing hours chatting to friends. They are also for people who spend too many evenings on their own but dislike the formality of joining a class or a club.

Knitting is a great leveller. We all begin with a pair of needles, a ball of wool – and a vision. The knitting, as is true of most repetitive activities, soon becomes automatic and we find that our minds relax and are freed up for conversation.

We become passengers on each other's train of thoughts.

Starting-up

Knitting groups have achieved almost cult status in the USA and the trend is growing into a worldwide phenomenon. Don't let that put you off the idea of starting up a new group though, because there is no shame in being part of something fashionable when it is also positive, non-competitive and, essentially, life enhancing.

The way you start a group will depend on where you live and how you spend the rest of your time. If you already know people who knit, try suggesting that you start a group together.

Designate one evening a week or fortnight as 'knitnight' with a change of venue each week from one home to another. The only requirement is comfy seats and enough elbow room to accommodate about 10 knitters. You do not need fees or agendas, simply arrive at any time after 7.30 and leave by 11.

Refreshments are optional and could be a glass of wine or juice to quench the thirst and a cup of tea or wickedly indulgent hot chocolate towards the end of the evening. Sometimes the numbers will swell and then shrink down to three or four, which will be quieter but no less enjoyable. There will be quiet moments when the only sound is that of clicking needles but more often than not there will be several animated conversations going on at the same time. And a lot of laughter!

Startup suggestions

1 Put a notice in your local wool shop window or a poster on a work, college or school noticeboard.

2 Join a knitting forum on the web, such as UK Handknitters (a Yahoo! group) or www. laughinghens.com where there are noticeboards with knitting-related news, ideas and topics for discussion. Put out feelers about knitting in your area via one of these.

3 Wear a homemade 'Join my knitting group badge' and wait for enquiries.

4 Advertise in the What's On section of your local paper.

5 Teach people you like to knit – supply a ball of wool and needles with stitches already cast on to make a garter stitch square for a blanket.

6 Approach a coffee shop or bar with the idea of a weekly or monthly knit-in.

7 Pick a day or evening that suits most of you most of the time. Be decisive but not too rigid – remember this is about having fun!

8 Don't over-recruit. If the group is to meet in members' homes, try to limit it to a number that most

can accommodate comfortably. Be flexible and inclusive though – there will be times when only a few can make it and this is an ideal time for a smaller home to be used.

9 Try to include a wide age range. Older members are likely to be more experienced and the younger ones more experimental and arty.

10 Support a charity knitting project. There are 'scarves for the homeless' and 'hats for the premature baby unit' projects in many cities. Once again, an online search will reveal a cause close to your heart. In our group, we knit simple baby vests for a Ugandan maternity hospital. This way everyone who joins has a garment to knit from day one.

Keeping it going

Once you have started a group and had a few get togethers, it will become clear that some core members will find it more convenient to host the evenings, while others look forward to getting out of the house. It is important that people feel neither put upon nor left out – the way we do it is to decide at the end of each knitnight where we will be the following week. We email, text or ring each other and pass the word around. Each of us takes the responsibility of finding out for herself and, that way, nobody feels left out.

You may find that you need more structure but we organize things in an instinctive female way and it works very well. When nobody is in charge, group decisions are quite easy. It's not a campaign you're planning – just some group knitting.

Warning

The great thing about knitting is that it isn't competitive but catering certainly can be. Stick to the basics and only deal with thirst not snacks. One glass of wine or water is all that's needed because our hands are knitting and our mouths are talking.

Author's experience

Initially we thought we might break for the summer but when summer came around it seemed too conventional an idea and we just carried on as usual. And, besides, we felt we would miss the group therapy!

Knitting tips and how to progress

- Once you feel comfortable with your knitting and have practised a variety of stitches, you will be ready to branch out and choose a pattern, buy the yarn and make something wonderful.

- Caution is urged! This is a make-or-break phase in your knitting future. It will be far more satisfying (and also less expensive) to knit simple garments successfully than to struggle with an over-ambitious pattern.

- Having to abandon a project is demoralizing but we have all done it – put it on top of the wardrobe for a rainy day or hand it in at a charity shop then start knitting something chunky for instant gratification.

- Certain things are not worth knitting. Buy a superfine cashmere sweater – it will be cheaper and look better than anything you can knit.

- Knit something for a charity – it will give you a nice warm feeling inside.

- Deadlines can kill your enthusiasm for knitting. Try not to promise anything for a special date – like Christmas – when you have quite enough to do already!

- It is easier to knit light colours than dark – especially at night when mistakes knitted in black are virtually invisible!

- When you knit with pale yarn, keep the balls in a clear plastic bag loosely gathered at the top with a rubber band. The yarn will stay clean even if it drops on the floor – as it inevitably will at some stage.

- Yarn is dipped into containers of dye and this causes slight variations in the same colour from the different dippings. Always buy enough yarn to complete the garment, rather than buying a bit at a time. Check that the dye lot numbers are the same – every ball of yarn has one.

- When knitting a striped scarf from oddments make sure that the different yarns are constructed from compatible fibres – for instance, all natural, all mixtures or all manmade fibres. Yarns behave in different ways when they are knitted up and, most importantly, when they are washed.

- Only substitute a large safety pin for a stitch holder for a small number of stitches or in an emergency. Safety pins can split the yarn and give you a nasty jab.

- Blocking and pressing: it will make all the difference if you don't rush this vital stage. Take your time and complete the sewing up with care and the results will speak for themselves.

- Buy shorter length needles for knitting on public transport. It will stop you poking the person next to you in the ribs.

- Left-handed beginners are best taught by other left-handed knitters.

- If the yarn doesn't slide easily along the needle, try running your needles through your hair. This adds the slightest coating of natural oil that will sort the problem out.

- Designate one evening a week as knitnight to knit, to sit and chat, and your friendships will grow with the rows while life stories unravel like balls of wool.

Online knitting community

There are thousands of knitting-related websites and blogs out there. Type the word 'knitting' into Google or Yahoo! and prepare to be amazed. You will find everything from the big name yarn suppliers to eBay store listings and individuals who simply want to share their enthusiasm and everything they know.

Search for 'knitting blogs' to bring up all the friendly small and quirky sites that often carry patterns and small ads from yarn suppliers.

Search for 'knitting patterns' to provide you with all the free patterns you will ever need.

Search for 'knitting yarns' for local and mail order suppliers.

Be inspired by *Vogue Knitting*, a US magazine with online news and book reviews: www.vogueknitting.com.

Yarn suppliers

Dragon Yarns
Online suppliers of interesting pure wool ranges such as British breeds and Bolivian alpacas
Website: www.dragonyarns.co.uk

Laughing Hens
Online ordering of yarns, patterns and equipment
Website features the latest and the best quality yarns and accessories
Website: www.laughinghens.com

Rowan Yarns
Quality natural yarns in gorgeous colours
Online knitting club and suppliers' information
Tel: 01484 681881
Website: www.knitrowan.com

Sirdar Yarns
Hand knitting and specialist yarns
General enquiries: enquiries@sirdar.co.uk
Nearest stockist: consumer@sirdar.co.uk

Twilleys of Stamford
Dishcloth cotton, denim yarn, lurex and chunky wool
Tel: 01780 752661
Email: twilleys@tbramsden.co.uk

The Yarn Warehouse
Online supplier of pure wool Aran and DK in lovely colour range
Website: www.yarnwarehouse.com

index